Pastel Painting

Red Housecoat

Pastel Painting

BY STEPHEN CSOKA

REINHOLD PUBLISHING CORPORATION/NEW YORK

ACKNOWLEDGMENT:
Special thanks to my friend, Ralph Fabri, N.A.,
whose invaluable help has made this book possible.

Designed by Ben Robinson
Type set by Howard O. Bullard, Inc.
Printed by the Comet Press, Inc.
Bound by Russell-Rutter Company, Inc.

To my wife, Margaret

CONTENTS

PREFACE

The word "pastel" generally suggests soft tones of pale and fragile colors. In the popular concept, pastel painting implies the use of these tones and colors, applied in a soft technique, for depicting appropriately delicate subject matter, like babies, lovely young women, dewy spring flowers. Many people consider the medium as well as the subject-matter weak and feminine; some, think, too, that the finished pastel painting is in itself fragile and transitory, ready to vanish from the face of the paper with a single puff of breath.

Fact and popular fiction are poles apart. True, pastels lend themselves particularly well to very light tones, but the range of color in this medium is exactly the same as in oil, watercolor, tempera and casein paintings. There is only one significant difference: in pastel painting we do not rely upon a dozen or so basic colors from which to mix all other colors and color values. We use, instead, pure pigments of a great many shades and tints prepared in the form of sticks. As an illustration, instead of mixing red and blue in order to obtain violet, and then white in varying quantities to obtain gradations of violet, as in other media, the pastel artist simply selects several shades of violet pastels, each a separate, ready-to-use stick. Any mixing or blending of colors is done directly on the paper.

The number of pastels to be used in a particular painting may range from one or two to several hundred different shades, and the range of effects obtainable with pastels is equally broad, limited only by the ability of the artist, and by his skill with the medium. An artist who creates individual, original work in oils is capable of being just as creative in pastels. It may seem easier to make a big noise with a trumpet than with a violin, but surely the violin can play great and powerful music.

As to the idea that pastel paintings are not permanent, this belief is at once wide-spread and erroneous. All art works, from pencil sketches to stone sculpture, can be destroyed by fire, flood or vandalism. Canvas can be cut and torn like paper; there is a solvent for every kind of paint. Admittedly, one can blow excessive pastel pigment off the paper; indeed, this is a technique employed to advantage by pastel artists. On the other hand, pastels are made from absolutely pure pigments and contain no ingredient that might fade, turn dark or otherwise deteriorate.

Pastels are much less expensive than other painting materials; they are also much more portable. No heavy paintbox to lug about, no costly brushes, no bottles of liquid to spill or break. Pastel paintings, adequately protected by an acetate cover, are completely transportable—and no need to wait for your picture to dry! In recent years, perfectly safe fixatives have been developed for protecting pastel paintings without altering the colors. When a pastel is framed, use a double-thick mat and glass to provide permanent protection; watercolors and caseins require the same safeguarding.

The variety of effects possible to achieve with pastels is almost limitless, and the artist who develops technical competence in the medium finds great satisfaction with it. Degas, undisputed master in pastels, loved them so much that he tried to make even his oil paintings look like pastels. An artist who normally paints in oil may, by the same token, be tempted to emulate the effect of oils when using pastels. But every medium has its own potentialities and its own limitations; one medium should not be used in an effort to obtain the inherent, natural effects of another medium. Oils should look like oils, and pastels like pastels. Only in this way can a given medium be exploited to the limit of its potentialities.

If you want to express yourself fully and fluently in any art medium, you must study and practice its techniques, just as you must study and practice a foreign language in order to express yourself with clarity and distinction in the newly acquired tongue. The purpose of this book is to provide basic information on the handling of all necessary tools and materials, and to investigate technical and artistic problems involved in pastel painting, including the choice of paper and colors, the selection of subject matter, the approach to composition, and the technique necessary for producing a work of art in pastel. The book presents you with the means; practice and experimentation will determine the extent of your success.

MATERIALS AND TOOLS

The invention of pastels as an art medium is popularly attributed to the German landscape painter, Johann Alexander Thiele (1685-1752). However, we have at least one pastel portrait by Guido Reni, an Italian artist who died forty-three years before Thiele was born. Thiele perfected the medium, but was overshadowed in its use by a contemporary, the Venetian Rosalba Carriera, about 160 of whose celebrated pastels are in the Dresden Museum collection. The eighteenth century Swiss artist, Jean Etienne Liotard, considered one of the greatest pastel painters, inspired many English artists when his works were exhibited at the Royal Academy, London, 1775.

The word "pastel" is derived from the paste into which the pigments are compounded before the sticks are molded. Pastel sticks are available in soft pastels and semi-hard pastels; recently, wood-encased pastel pencils have been offered on the market. Pastel pencils, manufactured in a variety of colors, are not to be confused with color crayons which contain a substantial quantity of wax.

Soft pastels are cylindrical sticks, wrapped in a paper sleeve, ready for use. The wrapper serves two purposes: it protects the stick, and contains the name and number of the color for handy reference. There are about sixty full-strength pastel colors; each of these comes in several darker and lighter values. Black, white and various tones of gray are

Sunflowers
This painting is a good example of the power one can achieve in pastels. I worked on chocolate-brown paper with soft pastels, using the side of the pastel for larger areas, the point for details. The star-shaped, round-centered flowers are contrasted with the straight-edged table, the squared red wall, the diagonal of the white tablecloth. The flowers are shown in front, back, side, and three-quarter views. They are also varied in size, and placed on different levels, to create movement and avoid monotony in the composition. The dark background eliminated the need for outlining each flower, stem and leaf, and contributed to the considerable depth of the picture.

included in the list. Darker shades of a pure pastel are produced by adding 15 to 40 percent dark pigments; lighter tints are made by adding 15 to 40 percent white. The complete palette of manufactured pastels available to the artist includes several hundred colors, shades and tints.

Semi-hard pastels, square in cross-section, have four flat sides, are sold without wrappers, and are available in about seventy-five colors. All pastels are sold in flat cardboard or wooden boxes with dividers separating the sticks. Keep your pastels in the boxes, in their original order, so that you will know just where each color is located, and won't have to fumble all over the box for the right stick. Soft pastels are marketed in assortments of 12 to 300 colors, semi-hard pastels are available in sets of 12 to 72 colors. You need not purchase the largest set to begin with, I recommend a starter set of 40 soft pastels; for sketching, a set of 24 may be adequate. As you become more skilled in the use of pastels, you will want to add colors to your palette. Semi-hard pastels are useful for drawing sharp, positive lines and fine details in colors; if you prefer to use only black for line drawing, buy a black pastel pencil.

In oil painting, a small group of colors can be intermixed to produce an infinite number of colors, shades, and tints. Pastels, however, cannot be mixed on the palette. It is possible to produce color gradations directly on a pastel painting by using one color over another; however, the best results are obtained by working directly with the right color in the right place. It is this precise selection and application of color that gives pastel its freshness, luminosity and brilliance.

Practically any paper with a "toothy" texture will hold pastel. Special pastel paper, plain or mounted, with a velvety (velour) finish, is particularly good for portrait work because it takes smooth blending easily. Sanded paper, also plain or mounted, is excellent for most subjects. If you like a rough, free style, use charcoal paper or watercolor paper. Rough paper gives pastel painting a loose, vibrating effect; it also takes well to lots of rubbing and scrubbing without loss of texture. Sketchbooks of charcoal paper and watercolor paper are available in many sizes. I recommend an 18 x 24 inch sketchbook of charcoal paper in assorted colors for outdoor sketching. Mounted paper is easier to handle, to store and to frame than unmounted sheets, but any paper can be mounted on heavy paperboard with a drop of white paste in each corner. Do not use rubber cement for this purpose, as it causes discoloration and does not stick permanently.

An extremely advantageous feature of pastel painting is the availability of paper in a wide range of colors, in addition to white, from palest gray or cream all the way to black. Select the color which is most suitable to your subject. Every scene and setting has a general over-all tone or color; a stormy day is gray, a sunny sky is blue, a fall landscape is predominantly rust-colored. An appropriately colored paper is helpful in establishing a prevailing mood, and eliminates a great deal of tedious background painting. White paper should be used, of course, when it is appropriate to the subject or mood, as in a snow-covered landscape.

If the extra-rough texture of watercolor paper appeals to you, but its whiteness does not, tint the paper with a watercolor wash of the desired color, before applying the pastels. Many of the "Old Masters" used tinted backgrounds for their work to establish a mood, or intensify a feeling of warmth or coolness in their paintings.

Canvas offers another satisfactory surface for the application of pastels. Two kinds are manufactured specifically for this medium, one with a velvety finish, the other with a sanded surface. Any good quality unbleached canvas having a smooth, even texture may be used if it is first treated with a thin coat of white shellac. The reverse side of primed oil painting canvas is usable, too, and offers the added advantage of protection against dampness when the pastel is framed. Canvas is available in practically any width and length, which enables you to work in a scale not limited by the size of manufactured pastel papers. However, it is wise to remember that pastels must be framed under glass, too large a size might make your framed picture very heavy and unwieldy.

In addition to pastels and paper or canvas, you will need the following items:
1) Paper stumps—pencil shaped, pointed rolls of soft paper used for blending fine lines and edges.
2) A very small, flat sable brush for blending the most delicate details.
3) Flat bristle brushes, 1/4- and 1/2-inch sizes, for rubbing off small areas of drawing before making chages or corrections.
4) A metal holder for semi-hard pastels.
5) A fixative spray for protecting and sealing your work. Modern fixatives do not change pastel colors; furthermore, it is possible to apply additional pastel over the fixative.
6) Protective sheets of heavy acetate, to be pasted over unframed pastels. Fasten acetate to corners of mat with masking tape.
7) Rags and paper tissues for rubbing pastel into large areas and for wiping hands.

The most talented artist is severely handicapped without the proper tools and materials. It may seem extravagant to buy the most expensive materials for your first pastel sketches; however, it is more difficult to work with poor equipment, and the beginner should not burden himself with this additional limitation. Cheap pastels have no covering power, cheap paper will not hold the pigment. There is a far greater difference in quality than in price between the least expensive and the most costly.

The illustrations show a variety of textures obtainable with different papers and pastels. Experiment with every possible kind of material in order to determine the advantages and disadvantages of each. Study the advertisements in art magazines to learn about new materials; through this experimentation and research, you will develop familiarity with the medium, its possibilities, and its limitations.

Field After Harvest
This preliminary sketch was drawn on white paper with brown semi-hard pastel. In a later painting made from the sketch, realistic colors were applied to each section as directly as possible. Various shades of green were used for delineating the trees; bluish tones defined the distant horizon; soft yellows in the center portion of the drawing indicated the millions of wheat stalks which remained after the harvesting machines had finished their work.

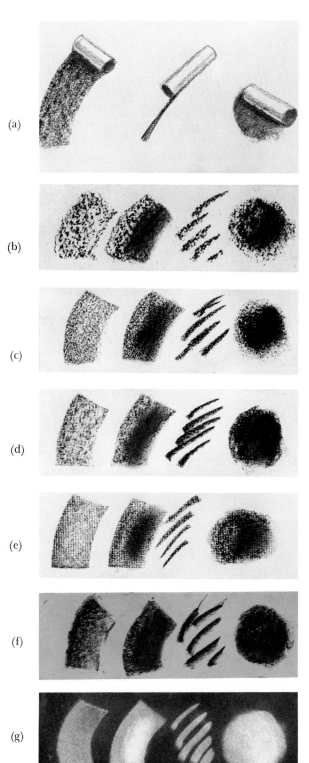

(a)

(b)

(c)

(d)

(e)

The grain of the paper greatly influences the appearance of the pastel stroke. On smooth paper, pastel spreads evenly and solidly, without breaks. A stroke on rough paper covers the ridges of the grain without filling the crevices, adding textural interest to the drawing. Select the paper best suited to your drawing style and to your subject. Shown here are

(a) flat strokes executed with the side of the pastel; linear strokes produced with the point; and rubbed-in tones. The same strokes are shown on

(b) 300-pound rough watercolor paper
(c) medium weight watercolor paper
(d) smooth drawing paper
(e) sanded paper
(f) charcoal paper
(g) velvet paper

(f)

(g)

15

Country Scene
Practically all the tools and materials normally used for pastel painting were employed in this picture. I worked on white paper, using soft pastels sideways. On larger sections, such as sky, walls, and the main bulk of the foliage, I rubbed the basic colors—blue, orange, and green—into the paper, using a different tissue for each color. The darker lines required semi-hard pastels of blue, brown and purple. I did not use black at all because I wanted a feeling of distance. To obtain sharper definition of the tree branches and the dilapidated barns, I sprayed the entire sketch with fixative before adding a few white spots—the shirt of the man, the house on the hillside, and the tail of a cow—and a few very strong lines as finishing touches.

In reference to fixatives, two facts should be remembered: (1) Too much fixative gives the painting an unpleasant sheen, so use fixative sparingly. (2) Although fixative gives a certain protection to the surface of the pastel, it does not prevent the possibility of scratching or rubbing off. When framing a painting, glass or acetate should be used to assure complete protection, and a heavy mat must separate the pastel from the glass or acetate.

16

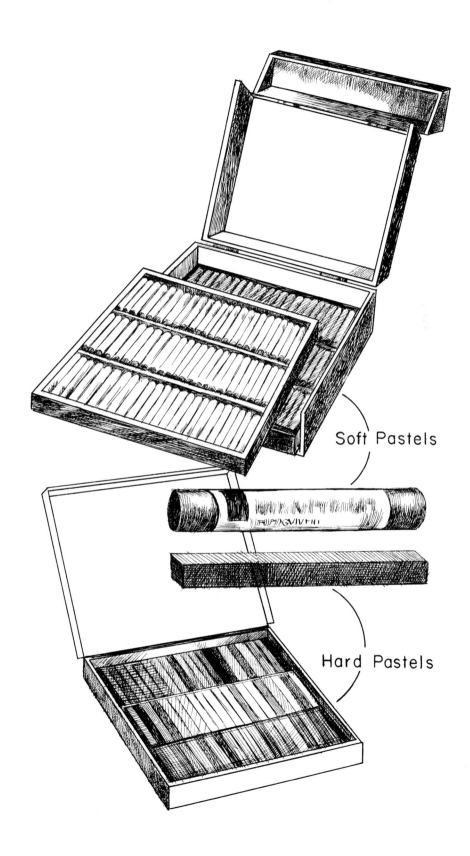

Soft Pastels

Hard Pastels

17

TECHNIQUES

When beginning a pastel painting, it is best to work first with soft pastels. Hold the stick lightly between thumb, index and middle fingers and apply the pigment in strokes, as if you were working with a brush. Use soft, broad strokes; do not attempt to make fine lines. Don't apply heavy pressure; pastel sticks break easily (save the broken pieces—they're perfectly usable).

Indicate large areas and forms, using the proper color wherever possible to avoid rubbing out and correcting later. Remember that you cannot paint a pure yellow over blue; the result will be green, rather than yellow. You can, however, turn blue into violet by working over it with carmine red, and you can obtain green by rubbing yellow into blue. Almost any color will turn lighter when white is rubbed into it; however, adding black is likely to make most colors look dirty rather than dark. Experimentation will show you that a darker green can be obtained by rubbing dark blue into a light green; dark purple makes red a little deeper; black will darken brown and blue. Delicate colors such as yellow, orange and vermilion can be made darker only by going over them with darker shades of the same colors.

Colors can be blended into each other with the fingertips, a paper stump, a rag, or tissue paper. To obtain a smooth, even effect, rub the pastel completely into the grain of the paper. Apply subsequent colors in such a manner that they adhere to the ridges and skip the valleys of the paper's surface. Details may be applied with soft pastel by wearing down a point or wedge-shaped tip on the stick; do not attempt to sharpen a pastel stick in any other manner. Whenever excessive pastel accumulates on the paper, remove the surplus by blowing it lightly, or by tapping the back of the paper before resuming your drawing. The basic pigments will adhere to the paper no matter how often you remove excessive pigment with these techniques.

The blending technique to be employed depends upon the subject

Polo Players

In this sketch, drawn on white paper while watching a polo game, I attempted to render the brilliant colors, the speed, action and excitement of the players on horseback. Nobody could possibly observe details in the fast, furious turns, twists and gestures of the players. I established the main forms with short pieces of pastels, using them flat, like brushes, and working with realistic colors. A few strokes suggest horses and men, legs and arms; dark lines indicate polo sticks and shadows. It is necessary to observe a game like polo closely for a time, in order to become familiar with typical gestures, poses and actions of the participants. It is impossible to sketch as rapidly as polo players move; however, sooner or later, actions are repeated, so you can return to earlier sketches for further drawing. This type of action sketching is admittedly difficult, but most rewarding.

and the size of the area to be blended. Most blending should be done with the fingertips. Use different fingers for different colors, and wipe your hands with tissues at frequent intervals. For small corners and lines, where the fingertip is too large a tool, use a paper stump, twisting it around in a constant circular motion so that it will wear down evenly. For the tiniest sections such as the delicate details in a portrait, use a small, flat sable brush. Color can also be applied with this brush; first rub a little pastel on a piece of rough paper, then pick up bits of the pigment on the tip of the brush.

Before making a correction, blow on the area you want to change, in order to remove excess pastel powder. If the section is small, brush it off gently with a flat bristle brush. The brush is less likely to damage the paper than a rag or a fingertip, as it removes the pastels without making the paper smooth. For fine details and finishing touches, work with semi-hard pastels, with which it is possible to make solid, fine lines. Semi-hard pastels can be sharpened to a fairly fine point with a razor-blade or a sandpaper block. Pastel pencils, too, are ideal for delicate details, and have the added advantage of keeping the fingers clean.

Fixative sprays provide a valuable technique for correcting pastel drawings. Spray the area to be corrected; the fixative will dry in a few seconds, holding down the pastel, so that additional pastel can be applied without stirring up underlying colors. This technique will also permit addition of sharp details, bright lines, deep shadows and sparkling highlights in pure colors. Many artists employ fixative in this way, even when there is no correction to be made, in order to obtain precise definition of forms. As in work with any art medium, experimentation, practice and careful observation of results are vitally important.

SKETCHING

A brief glance at great art of the past and present will furnish proof of the value of sketching in terms of the quality of the finished work of art. With only two notable exceptions in the history of fine art, preliminary sketching has been an essential element of esthetic discipline traditionally accepted and practiced by the artist. The *Dadaist* movement, an outgrowth of World War I, discarded sketching, along with all other forms of discipline, and expressed contempt for the world. More recently, the *Abstract-Expressionist* artists have worked directly, without preliminary sketching, in an effort to achieve spontaneous expression. Outside of these two groups, artists have customarily approached their work with a considerable degree of care and forethought.

It is distressing to realize, after many hours of work on a picture, that something is basically wrong with it. After such a large investment in time and effort, it is difficult to wipe off your work, or tear it up and begin again. Such drastic steps can be avoided with preliminary sketching. Ideas are born and clarified while you sketch; it is much less discouraging to discard a quick, small-scale sketch than to attempt to correct a detailed, large-scale painting. With pastels as with other media, continuous changing is likely to produce only chaos.

Sketches are the shorthand notes of the artist. They can be products of the artist's imagination, or graphic records of the artist's visual experience, drawn with direct reference to an actual person, place or thing. Develop the habit of sketching; carry paper, pencil and a small packet of pastels with you wherever you go, and use them whenever you see anything worth sketching, or to sketch an idea you may want to develop at a later date. A few lines jotted down at the time will refresh your memory.

Sketching is important because it trains you to observe, and helps you to become familiar with your subject. Study your sketches a few days

S. Cirker

View of Lake Huntington
Step 1. Hills and general earth contours are indicated with a few sketchy lines. Sufficient space is retained for foreground details.
Step 2. The more prominent trees, shrubs and other landscape elements are added in outline form.
Step 3. Greater definition is given to all forms; larger masses of shadow are indicated. The resulting sketch contains sufficient reference material for later development into a finished painting, through the addition of realistic colors and greater detail. This sketch was drawn on white paper with semi-hard brown pastel.

Wild Apple Tree
I sketched this attractive tree because I thought it might be useful in some future composition. It was done with black pastel pencil on warm gray paper. The colors of paper and pastel are of little significance in one-color sketches, except insofar as they provide sufficient contrast. However, it is worthwhile trying various combinations, in order to study the results produced.

23

after making them; you will then be able to evaluate them more objectively. You will often find that a combination of elements taken from several different sketches will produce a well-balanced, cohesive drawing. In landscape painting, it is often advantageous to develop a final color plan from sketches, rather than from reference to the actual scene. The setting may not have the ideal illumination at precisely the moment you are present; lights and shadows may be too hazy, or too sharp. Tonal qualities are altered by the brightness of the sun; color intensities change with the hour of day. It is not possible to detach yourself from what you see on the spot; later on, with your sketches for reference, you can alter the effect of light and shadow to emphasize the most important features of your painting, and plan your color to achieve the desired mood.

With these possibilities in mind, make several sketches; study your subject from several different angles, and make sketched notes from different viewpoints. Make individual studies, too, of an unusual rock or tree, a charming farmhouse. Pastel sketching requires very little time, and absolutely no preparation of materials—no easel to set up, no colors to squeeze upon a palette, no liquids to pour. All you need is a sketchbook in assorted colors, and a flat box to hold your pastels.

You may sketch in one color, or with a limited palette of three or four colors, or with a complete range of colors, depending upon your purpose. Full color is advisable for a complicated theme; a single dark pastel is preferable for individual studies where detailed forms are more important than realistic color.

When making a detailed sketch in a single color, use the pastel stick sometimes as a pencil with a beveled edge and sometimes as a brush. Work with a sharp tip when fine lines are required; hold the stick flat for applying tone to a large area. If you work with a limited palette of one dark color and a few light ones, emphasize strong contrasts rather than subtle nuances. In the full-color approach, try to apply the colors you actually see, beginning with the background and working forward. Add trees, bushes, other objects and lines in the right places, in correct proportions, omitting fine details.

Indoor sketching serves the same fundamental purpose as outdoor sketching. The corner of a room can make an attractive picture by itself, or it can become a good background for a more complicated composition. People behave differently indoors than they do outdoors; their movements are slower, more restrained. The interplay of light and shadow is also very different indoors; contrasts are not so great, except when powerful artificial light is employed. The problems of perspective are normally more evident in a drawing of an interior than in a landscape study; furnishings and architecture must be studied and rendered realistically in order to be convincing. When using an interior for either the subject or the background of a painting, it is advisable to do a preliminary outline drawing, in correct perspective, before applying color.

When sketching figures or objects in motion, it is essential first to become familiar with the subject, with its form and typical movements or gestures, through careful observation. This is particularly important when preparing to sketch an unfamiliar object, or an action which you have seldom, or never, witnessed before. Even if you never utilize such a sketch, and even if the subject seems uninteresting to the casual observer, the knowledge and skill you derive from its execution will be of value to you for other paintings. While sketching, you will become more aware of the problems presented by your specific subject, but at the same time you will train your eye to observe—an invaluable lesson

Driftwood
This piece of twisted tree-trunk captured my imagination. I sketched it in dark gray semi-hard pastel on light gray paper, emphasizing its resemblance to a strange, tentacled animal. Color and background were incidental to the drawing; the gnarled, writhing branches alone drew me to the subject. This sketch was used later in the painting, *Seascape,* shown on page 43.

which will carry over into all your art work.

Concentrate on recording the essentials: composition, proportions, predominant colors, highlights and shadows, general mood. Details are easy to add, once you have the main forms under control. Fine details should be the finishing touches of your painting; any details drawn during the early stages are bound to be obliterated as you keep painting and changing. A finished pastel painting based on good sketches and logical step-by-step development is bound to reflect the care with which it was done; a haphazard approach will almost inevitably produce haphazard results.

The Jury
The warm tone of the room suggested the use of a rust-colored charcoal paper to establish both background and mood for this painting. I reduced the figures in scale to emphasize the largeness of the hall. Before sketching, I watched the jury members as they walked back and forth in the art gallery, scrutinizing the pictures in preparation for making their final decision. This is not an easily recognized, every-day subject; compositions of this sort require much preliminary study for successful results.

COMPOSITION

According to Webster's Dictionary, the word "composition" is defined as, "The art or practice of so combining the parts of a work of art as to produce a harmonious whole." "Harmony," in turn, is generally defined as an agreement between the parts of a design or composition giving unity of effect or an esthetic whole. In other words, composition is a deliberately planned design which holds a work together in such a manner that no part of the work can be changed, moved or eliminated without destroying or greatly disturbing the total effect.

In contemporary art, however, there are artists who throw, drip or squirt paint on canvas automatically, calling the results of this "self-expression" art. If this were true, any child could be a fine artist. A pleasing color combination or an unusual pattern may be quite acceptable as a design for wallpaper or textiles, but not as a work of art. Such a design has no composition; it is conceived as an over-all pattern which has no beginning and no end. It can be cut off anywhere without damaging its decorative quality.

Most artists agree that novel or odd techniques can lead to artistic results only if certain fundamental principles are observed. Probably the most vital of these is composition. Today, it is not at all necessary to tell a story in a picture, as was done in the biblical, mythological or historical paintings of the past. Nor is it necessary, or even desirable, to make every detail photographically precise. Nevertheless, the word "Art" still denotes a carefully planned creative work, rather than an accident.

A composition can be traditional or modern. It can be non-representational, that is, having no recognizable subject matter. It still remains a composition, so long as it has been deliberately planned and executed in order to make a pictorial entity of pattern and color. Although compositional theory has been changed by history, it has remained unaltered by geography; the basic principles of composition are virtually

Dancing Figures

Step 1. (Top) Figures were first indicated in black outline form; action lines and main masses were sketched in roughly. Then quick dashes of flesh-toned pastels were applied— light tones for the foreground figures, darker tones for the figures in the distance. I soon became aware of several compositional errors. The figures were too large and appeared crowded; the woman at the far right seemed to have entered the picture by accident, while the form at left had barely enough room to move. The contrast between the nudes in the foreground and those in the distance was not sharp enough, and the background tones appeared weak and faded.

Step 2. (Bottom) In the revised composition, the figures are relatively smaller, suggesting spaciousness. The forms at right and left curve inward to give the composition unity. The darkened flesh-tones of the figures in the distance emphasize depth, while the red tones in the background lend warmth to the figures.

28

the same in all parts of the world. The Greeks and Romans of antiquity and the Renaissance artists of the fifteenth and sixteenth centuries preferred symmetrical balance in art. In the Baroque period of the seventeenth and eighteenth centuries, this meticulous balance yielded to an asymmetrical, diagonal arrangement which remains the most generally accepted standard today. The same evolution in compositional theory can be noticed in the works of Far East artists. In every age and country, the composition of a painting has had to include the entire subject, like a scene on a stage. The most important features are given prominence; the balance is subdued but not neglected. In photographs, figures or objects are often cut off in an odd, sometimes ridiculous manner. The camera cannot think or select; it can only record everything within the range of its lens. The artist, however, must be able to visualize the final appearance of his work even before he begins to paint. If the artist's purpose involved nothing more than the creation of a photographic likeness, the development of the camera would have brought about the extinction of the artist. It is the artist's aim to create an esthetic picture, not a photographic image; he accomplishes this by arranging and rearranging his subject matter until he manipulates the material into a pleasing, interesting composition.

An artist working from imagination usually has a shape in mind, as well as an idea, for a painting. Since the edges of the paper itself form the external boundaries of the composition, it is important to determine the right shape for your painting before beginning to draw. One method is to cut a piece of paper in the shape you have in mind, on a much smaller scale but in the correct proportions, and begin composing on this, in a sketchy style. When you feel your paper can't take any more alterations, begin a new sketch, in a different shape, just to make sure you are on the right track. You may find that your subject looks better in a horizontal shape than in a vertical one, or that a long, narrow rectangle enhances the mood of your subject better than the squarish shape of an earlier sketch. Omit details from all preliminary composition-sketches; they are nonessential at this stage of your work, and contribute nothing toward the solution of composition problems.

Here is a lesson plan which will help you to learn to sketch and compose at the same time. First, select a subject which appeals to you—one that has numerous elements, a broad view of farmland, for example. It has patches of vegetation and soil, roads, trees, bushes, buildings, hills, sky and clouds. Your problem is to decide what combination of these elements will make the view interesting, dramatic, or mood-evocative. By telescoping, that is, by pushing various parts of the actual scenery together, by moving a lovely tree from far left to right, by making one object larger, another one smaller than it really is, you can assemble all the elements of your subject into a pleasing picture. Your sketch will be realistic; it will contain all the essential details; it will resemble the portion of landscape you observed while drawing, but it will not be a photographic image.

Make plenty of sketches on the spot, and later, select the best features of each for a final composition. After sufficient practice, you will be able to sketch and compose simultaneously. Study the scenery carefully for a few minutes without drawing. Then try to visualize the changes that would make the view more artistic. Now begin to sketch, incorporating these changes into your drawing. Practice this exercise; with experience, simultaneous sketching and composing will soon become a familiar procedure, and an invaluable aid to your work in any medium.

Descent from the Cross
Step 1. (Top, facing page) In an imaginative figure composition, the parts and postures of the bodies must be used as abstract design elements combined in a cohesive pattern. Indicate this pattern with a few straight and curved lines before developing any detail.
Step 2. (Bottom, facing page) Once you are satisfied with the lineal design, add details gradually, working from large to small. Your composition will be easier to alter at the sketch stage than after parts have been drawn in detail.
Step 3. (Above) The completed work has color, depth, shadows, lights; faces are detailed to show expression. Forms can be emphasized with stronger outlines in dark, semi-hard pastels in colors selected to harmonize with the areas you want to accent.

Landscape with Cows

As a young boy, I saw so many cows that I
could not imagine a landscape without these
placid, slow-moving creatures. I wanted to stress
this in my final drawing; to paint cows as an
artistic subject, not as an illustration for a book
of natural history. In the final composition
shown here, the cows are placed in almost
symmetrical balance; one standing quietly on
higher ground, the other in motion, grazing below. The composition has a diagonal, off-
centered design, strengthened by the whiteness
of the standing cow above the brown-and-buff
tones of the grazing animal. The design is
further accented by dark shadows at the center
of the foreground. Horizontal clouds emphasize
the flatness of the countryside, while the warm
gray paper establishes the mood of a mild,
rainy day in autumn.

Three of the many sketches made before a satisfactory composition was produced are shown at
the right and on the facing page. It is easy to

paint a large landscape inhabited by small
cows; however, I wished to emphasize the animals and minimize the setting. Their positions,
motions and colors were far more important to
my drawing than the surrounding scenery. I believe the final solution, above, is superior to
any of the preliminary sketches.

LANDSCAPES

Landscapes are the most popular subjects in the pictorial arts, and with good reason. In a fast-moving, mechanized, industrialized world, the tranquil countryside, rich in its ever-changing colors, gives us renewed vigor and strength. There is something relaxing as well as exhilarating in the unspoiled beauty of nature, particularly for people who live in tense, crowded cities. The landscape is associated in their minds with vacation, leisure, informality, and release from the restraints of urban living. And what nicer way is there to bring this peacefulness back home than through the landscape drawings you have created!

A sketchbook of charcoal paper in assorted colors, a box of pastels, a small folding stool, and you are prepared to paint any setting that catches your fancy. Don't worry about smearing your pastel paintings; they can be protected easily. When you go out into the countryside for a sketching session, carry along several sheets of acetate, the same size as your sketchbook. When you complete a sketch, leave it in your sketchbook, place an acetate sheet over it, and proceed with the next sketch. When you return home, you can remove your drawings from the sketchbook and store them, with their acetate covers, in a portfolio or drawer.

34

TREES: It is impossible to draw a convincing landscape without knowing how to draw realistic, recognizable trees. There are innumerable species of trees, and within each species, every tree is different. Trunks, branches, leaves, colors, proportions, bark, lights and shadows must be carefully observed, and meticulously rendered.

Trees are easier to study in the fall, winter and early spring, when their anatomical structure is exposed, than when covered with summer foliage. The same trees should be studied and sketched throughout the year, from season to season, in order to obtain a true understanding of their features, and their characteristic appearance during each season of the year.

The average tree is well-balanced, and fairly symmetrical in shape; it would topple over if leaves and branches were not quite evenly distributed. Trees exposed to strong winds are likely to acquire odd, twisted, gnarled shapes; and instead of growing straight, will have a characteristic lean in the direction of the prevailing winds. When beginning your tree studies, first observe only the trunk and the main branches. Render these in correct proportions and shapes. Then begin to develop the smaller branches which radiate from the large ones; observe their directions and proportions, the manner in which they are fastened to, and grow out of, the main branches. The main branches form the skeleton of the tree, and should be indicated, even when the tree is drawn in full foliage.

Each species of tree has its own characteristic type of foliage. Observe

Squall on the Lake
(Facing page, top.) While I was admiring this little lake, a storm rolled up unexpectedly. On the blue-gray paper, I needed only a few darker spots for the clouds. With brown and black semi-hard pastels, I indicated the trees bent by the squall. Note that the wind bent them in the same direction. A stormy scene must be drawn rapidly because everything changes constantly; the mood, rather than the image, must be captured. My son and daughter headed homeward on their bicycles to escape the approaching rain. I jotted them down quickly, with oval strokes for the bicycle wheels, and a few dashes of bright color for the garments. There are no delicate details; these figures are not standing still.

Winter Scenery
(Facing page, bottom.) I worked on rough, white, watercolor paper, appropriate for the subject. After sketching the small houses, barren trees and fences in dark lines, I added the gay colors characteristic of country houses. Rough paper causes the colors to vibrate and glow, and helped me to create a picture of a dry, sparkling winter day.

35

the general outlines of the foliage mass, and its division into smaller, similarly shaped sections. Consider lights and shadows while sketching; note the variety of greens—yellowish, bluish, brownish, grayish. Without attempting to paint individual leaves, try to indicate that the foliage is not a solid mass; birds can fly between the leaves and branches, and sunlight can filter down. Use small, flat pieces of pastel for the main masses and colors; apply short strokes or dots over these with the pointed ends. By employing several different shades of greens in the short strokes, you can reproduce the lacy, vibrant texture characteristic of foliage. Where roots are visible, observe them with as much care as the rest of the tree. Such roots often take on fascinating twisted shapes.

Early Spring
When drawing or painting trees, study the trunks and main branches carefully. One branch grows out of another, not in haphazard fashion, but according to the rules of nature.

Look under the foliage to see the full skeleton of the tree. Semi-hard pastels or pastel pencils are good for such studies. Paint the general outlines and the most obvious masses of foliage; pay no attention to individual leaves.

Tree Study
Although no two trees are ever exactly alike, trees of the same species have recognizable similarities, and the characteristic features belonging to the species. These family traits appear in all of nature; studies like the one shown here will help you to observe them.

Fig Trees
I never miss an opportunity to draw trees with which I am not familiar. One seldom encounters fig trees in American cities; I sketched these for future reference.

Sketch single trees, clusters of trees, whole forests. Draw trees in their heavy foliage of summer and their bleak barrenness of winter. Study massive trees bent with age, and tender saplings struggling for life. Paint a tree-filled landscape at the height of a storm; do the same scene after the storm has passed, when the trees are bathed in benign sunlight. A tree can be a very stimulating subject for a painting all by itself. Handsome, well-drawn trees add immeasurably to the pictorial value of an outdoor painting.

Trees

I used white paper for this painting because I
wanted the white clouds to contrast with the
darker foliage. First I applied flat greenish
tones for the areas in the distance, using short
pieces of pastel held edgewise. Then I added
burnt sienna, cobalt blue, ultramarine blue,
ochre and orange, to give rich variety of tone
to the foliage. The tree-trunks were dashed off
in dark blue, brown, and black strokes of semi-
hard pastels. I left the foreground empty to
give a feeling of rest, as if it were a clearing in
the woods. Large areas of white paper were left
exposed in the sky, creating an atmosphere of
brilliance. While this painting is realistic
enough, it is by no means a direct, photographic image of what I actually saw. It is,
instead, a synthesis of foliage, tree trunks, and
colors used to create a feeling, as well as a picture, of a pleasant, inviting forest area.

Gnarled Trees
This drawing is in brown pastel on yellow ochre paper. The trees appear animated, ready to jump out of the ground. In such studies, the background is unimportant, but the shapes of the trees, the roots, and the manner in which the trees grow out of the ground should be carefully observed.

FARMS AND BARNS: Although many American farms are modern, spic-and-span, highly-mechanized enterprises, we still have plenty of the old-fashioned, rustic, traditional farms, with enough barns, sheds, silos, stables and chicken coops to provide the artists with countless pictorial themes.

Farm buildings often ramble over large areas, and would appear very small in relation to the surrounding landscape if painted with absolute realism. By telescoping the many units of a farm complex, pushing various structures closer together, you can give the main subject greater prominence. An old shed, sun-baked and weather-worn, may be the most picturesque feature on a farm; a large-scale study of this single building would make an interesting pastel drawing. Observe the weather-beaten planks or clapboards, the patched roof, the rickety door on rusty hinges, the cracked or missing windowpanes.

An old barn is usually a delightful subject for textural effects. The grain and knots of the wood, the shingles, tarpaper and other materials, the dirt at the base of the walls, the road leading to the shed, the grass,

39

Photograph of a Barn

Snapshots can be very helpful to even the most experienced artist. If you have good photographs, have them enlarged sufficiently so that details are distinguishable. Then you may use them as reference for painting. Avoid exact copying; improve on the photograph's composition by shifting and rearranging the elements of the landscape.

Pastel from a Photograph

In the painting, I reduced the length of the barn, and therefore increased the apparent height. I moved the farm machinery from the left corner of the barn to the front, and turned the small closed substructure into an open shed. The trees are closer to each other and to the barn, than they appear in the photograph. The sky area is larger; a dark cloud fills the right side, casting a shadow on the earth. I gave the flat, monotonous foreground a more complicated pattern of hill, road and field, with a much greater variety of colors.

40

Long Island Barn
The light buff paper gave me an ideal foundation for the orange-colored barn, the dirt road, and much of the foreground. The bright blue sky contrasts dramatically with the vivid orange barn. Uneven, sagging planks, accented by out-lines, stress the barn's dilapidated condition. Dark violet shadows enhance the brilliance of the orange walls. A flock of white and gray pigeons above the roof lends an extra touch of life to the scene.

weeds, stones, scraps of wood and corroded odds and ends which usually collect about the barn—these can delight the observer and inspire the artist to paint a captivating picture.

Even if the buildings in your painting are small, their age, state of deterioration, characteristic appearance of friendly warmth should be reflected in your work. Pastels lend themselves to this kind of emphasis. Semi-hard pastels are a must for the finer details. When working on a fairly large scale, try to depict the intricate natural design of the grain on weather-beaten wood planks, the delicate shading of rain-washed, sun-scorched walls, the scrubby look of weeds near the buildings.

From the farmer's viewpoint, an up-to-date, freshly painted barn would make a prettier picture. The artist, however, finds much more challenge and delight in drawing dilapidated shacks and sheds. At any rate, be sure to ask the farmer's permission before beginning to sketch, particularly if you must trespass on his property. Explain to him that you are sketching for pleasure, not for money; be sure to show him your finished work.

The farm landscape—hills, trees, planted or plowed lands—should be composed in such a manner that structures and their settings are related to each other in size, color and technique. It is incongruous to paint highly detailed trees while indicating buildings in a patchy, crude manner. It is just as illogical to paint every minute detail of a barn, and then surround it with a few splotches of green to suggest trees. Balance your style throughout the picture; ultimately, all parts of a painting are of equal significance. One slapdash, unfinished section makes the entire drawing appear messy and incomplete. No work of art can be considered finished until every part of it is carried to the same level of execution.

SEASCAPES: Calm water, like a mirror, reflects images. The reflection in the water is slightly bluish or greenish in tone, and usually somewhat lighter than the actual scene or object. When the water's surface is rippled by a passing breeze, the image is blurred; the reflection disappears completely in choppy water. The main colors of even the stormiest waters are influenced by sun, sky and clouds; the sea is never a single, flat tone. Its colors range from the white foam of the waves through greens, violets, light blues to an almost ink-blue shade. Pastels are ideal for the rendering of these subtle, changing colors; they can be applied to your drawing as rapidly as the colors in nature change. There is no wet paint, no-premixing of the correct shade, no muddiness. Pure colors are applied and blended directly on the painting.

Select the right paper for the over-all effect of your seascape—blue for a sunny sky, gray for a cloudy one. Use green if you are planning to paint a large expanse of water, white if there are white clouds in the sky and foam-capped waves in the ocean. Observe, first of all, the position of the horizon. On the open sea, the horizon is exactly where water and sky meet. When seen from a point along the shore, the horizon is lower than when viewed from a more elevated position. The higher the viewpoint, the larger the water area. When rendering a hilly shoreline, a higher viewpoint will reveal more of the pattern of hills. If, however,

Seascape with Driftwood
This painting is a characteristic example of the liberties an artist must take with his subject matter, to improve upon nature. The view of a wind-swept sea was turned into a more com-plicated picture by the introduction of two brightly-clad figures and a twisted, broken tree-trunk. The driftwood and the people give scale to the ocean, and make the scene more dramatic and imaginative.

you wish to emphasize the vast expanse of sky, place the horizon lower. In any event, avoid placing the horizon in the center of the paper; the resulting equal division of sky and water is monotonous.

Rub the main colors into the paper with a tissue or stump and keep your fingers clean for the more delicate work ahead. Draw your colors in directly; if parts of the sea are Nile green, light violet, pale blue, apply the right pastel stick for each. You can apply one color over another, but remember that it is always easier to make a pastel color lighter than darker. Black or other dark strokes can be applied anywhere to underscore and emphasize certain forms. However, if you wish to darken an entire section of your drawing, dust off that portion with a bristle brush before applying the darker tones. Brilliant accents can be added to a dark area by stroking the lighter tones in gently, merely touching the surface of the paper with the soft pastel stick.

Rocks in Maine

The boulders in this seaside setting suggested the use of ochre-colored charcoal paper. The dark portions of the rocks are drawn in black, brown, purple and dark green, while the lighter areas are represented almost entirely by the color of the paper itself. The sky is deep blue and gray, with violet streaks near the horizon, emphasizing distance. The sea is ultramarine blue and Nile green. I sprayed the painting several times in order to obtain the dark tones in the rocks, and the sparkling white foam of the surf.

Lighthouse

In rendering a subject like this, shapes and proportions of the main structures must be carefully observed. Composition, too, should be precisely planned. If the lighthouse had been placed in the exact center of the paper, the picture would have been dull and monotonous. The shore and rocks are important elements in the design; take liberties with the shapes and placement of such objects to heighten the impact of your pictures.

Sand Pits

I painted this seascape from a hill-top in order to show the vast expanse of the pits. The blue-gray paper emphasizes the brightness of the sunlight on the sand hills. Using the color of the paper for most of the background, I added only a few strokes of blue to the sky, a little blue and green to the water, and some burnt sienna shading to the hills and buildings.

In seascapes as in other subjects, you have the artist's prerogative to change nature by shifting, eliminating, or adding elements to make your work richer, more interesting from a pictorial viewpoint. Very often, the addition of one or two judiciously selected elements can heighten the dramatic impact of a picture. For example, an empty stretch of beach appears even lonelier with the addition of a single, small figure walking along the shore. A pounding surf is given added scale and strength when contrasted with some small, fragile object, like a tiny boat struggling for shore, or a pair of gulls flying overhead.

CITYSCAPES: Houses, castles, churches, ruins, quiet village streets and bustling city scenes provide a vast storehouse of pictorial subject matter. Decayed castles and historical ruins are rather scarce in the United States, but other architectural subjects abound wherever people live, and work, and pray. Skyscrapers are as inspiring to some artists as old churches or quaint Victorian houses are to others. Buildings in the process of construction or demolition, alive with scaffolds, cranes, machines, and laborers, are a favorite theme of many artists, while village market places, with their colorful fruit and vegetable stalls, gay awnings, and busy shoppers, furnish inspiration for others.

Few present-day artists attempt to paint every window, brick and shingle in minute detail. Emphasis is more often placed on the picturesque effect of buildings, the movement of pedestrians and vehicles, the general atmosphere of the view. The artist is more interested in depicting the glistening grayness of a rainy day in the city, peopled with scurrying, umbrella-carrying pedestrians dodging between rain-shiny automobiles; a radiant sunset, with its blues and golds reflected in glass-walled skyscrapers; or a small-town street at dusk, with mellow light flickering at the windows of stately old houses.

The houses of a small village, nestled among huge trees, present a

Street Corner
The subject of this painting is an old Victorian house, altered to suit new business tenants, yet retaining the flavor of earlier days, with its imposing stoop and big shade trees. In the foreground, men are working in a manhole, protected by yellow stanchions and a portable metal fence. Since no single color dominated the setting, I used white paper for the painting.

Broken Wall
In this composition, I tried to capture the feeling of change. Old houses are demolished to make way for modern buildings. For a brief period between the old and the new, these relics resemble the ruins of the Old World. Brick and broken plaster, remnants of paint and wallpaper add to the artistic effect.

46

charming subject for the artist, but big-city boulevards provide 'a greater variety of architectural forms. Old and new buildings, large and small, stand side by side. They are built of every conceivable material—brick, stucco, wood, stone, marble, aluminum, steel, glass—in a wide range of colors. Neon lights glow in the evening, adding fabulous hues to the cityscape; the color of the sky changes with the time of day, altering the tones of the entire panorama.

The successful rendering of cityscapes is dependent upon extensive preliminary sketching and study of architectural details. You will have no difficulty locating subjects for sketching; any city street will provide you with source material for hour after hour of study. I live in a quiet neighborhood of one- and two-family houses; just around the corner the cityscape changes radically into broad avenues congested with traffic, lined on both sides with a fascinating assortment of buildings from the turn of the century. These houses present an incredible conglomeration of pretentious entrances, crenelated roofs, jig-saw cornices, fancy ironwork and nonsensical ornamentation. Age has imbued them with a quaint, humorous charm that makes them poetic as well as picturesque. There is no mechanical repetition here, no sterile mass-production. Each structure is unique in materials and color as well as in design.

No matter where you live, you should be able to find something in your surroundings that intrigues you and arouses your desire to paint. Respond to this inspiration with a series of sketches and detail studies; when you have probed your subject thoroughly in this manner, you will be equipped to begin a serious cityscape. Use semi-hard pastels for laying out your sketches, soft pastels for blocking in main color areas.

These sketching sessions will help you to develop the ability to observe, and the skill to render accurate proportions and colors. However, a basic knowledge of the essential rules of perspective is absolutely necessary for rendering cityscapes. These rules are explained in the following chapter.

PERSPECTIVE

Every object, whatever its size, is three dimensional; it has height, width and depth. The painter depicts these three-dimensional objects on a flat, two-dimensional surface—a wall, a board, canvas or paper. Nevertheless he can make his subjects appear three-dimensional by following the rules of perspective. The ancient Greeks had an excellent understanding of perspective theory; the wall paintings of Pompeii prove that Roman artists also knew a great deal about perspective. The Renaissance and Baroque artists became absolute masters of perspective, and succeeded in creating a perfect illusion of three-dimensional space in their paintings.

Perspective is not an optical trick; it is based on observation, not of the measured dimensions of each object, but of the visual appearance of each object. A square is visually a square only when observed directly from the front. When you move to its right or left, above or below it, it ceases to look like a square. A disk is round only when viewed from the front, it appears elliptical from any other direction, becoming narrower and narrower as you move away from it. If we look down a long corridor lined on both sides with arches, all exactly the same size and shape, the arch nearest to us appears largest, the others seem to diminish in size according to their distance from our eyes. Every object appears smaller and smaller as it recedes in space. This is why we can see a large part of a city, or a panoramic landscape, through the frame of a small window.

In order to give the illusion of space to a drawing or painting, we must represent each object in perspective. We do not paint it in its actual shape, but in the distorted form in which it appears to our eyes. The camera has a lens, a mechanical eye which reproduces what it sees without thinking. But the human eye is linked with a brain which refuses to accept what it fails to comprehend. The average man, unschooled in the laws of perspective, does not understand how and why a ten-story building in the distance should be drawn smaller than a two-story house in the foreground. Nor can he understand the perspective distortions of shapes described previously.

Although photographic precision is not their objective, most artists still base their works on reality, painting in a representational manner. Even though much of our contemporary art is a departure from absolute three-dimensional reality, a knowledge of perspective is essential, particularly for artists who work with architectural subjects. Thus far, we have referred only to linear perspective, the change in shape and the diminution of size according to the position and distance of an object in relation to the observer. The artist is also concerned with color perspective, which often makes colors appear lighter and hazier as the distance between the object and the eye increases. A full three-dimensional effect can be achieved only through the correct rendering in perspective of lines, shapes, colors, lights and shadows.

The first rule to remember in linear perspective is that all parallel, horizontal lines in a given plane converge at one point on the horizon. For example, railroad tracks, telegraph wires, roads going in the same

direction, appear to come together on the horizon, at a single spot, called the Vanishing Point. Hold a yardstick horizontally in front of your eyes; all parallel lines below the yardstick will appear to converge upward as they recede in the distance, while all parallel lines above the yardstick appear to converge downward. From an elevated viewpoint, such as a mountaintop, or an observation tower, the horizon appears much higher; therefore, we see a much larger area below it, and correspondingly less sky above it. From a lower viewpoint, the horizon is much lower; we see much less area below the horizon, and that much more above it.

All parallel lines in the same plane have the same vanishing point; but there is a separate vanishing point for each group of parallel lines. As a simple illustration to clarify this statement, try to visualize the floor lines of a sky-scraper. All the floor-lines on the front wall (a single plane) of the building converge in one vanishing point. All similar lines on the side wall of the same building (another plane) run into another vanishing point. Both of these vanishing points are on the same horizon.

Albrecht Dürer and other Renaissance masters used a simple device for observing perspective accurately. They drew vertical and horizontal lines about half-an-inch apart on a piece of glass, and viewed their subject matter through this "finder," in order to determine the visual direction of each line, the visual size and shape of each object in relation to the squares on the finder. We can duplicate this device by squaring up a 3″ x 4″ piece of heavy acetate and mounting it in a cardboard mat cut to size. This simple "finder" is also helpful in selecting and composing an outdoor subject. Close one eye; hold the finder in front of the other eye and move it back and forth until you find the most attractive view of the landscape. The squared viewer will also help you in blocking out your sketch. The viewer is not essential; you can compare visual lines with imaginary verticals and horizontals. One way or another, you must learn how to see three-dimensional reality as it will appear when reduced to a two-dimensional picture. With practice, perspective becomes as simple as sharpening a pencil.

Vertical lines usually remain vertical, but horizontal lines usually appear to go upward if they are below the horizon, and downward if above it. Parallel horizontal lines receding from the eye appear to be running into a single point, called the vanishing point, on the horizon. This convergence of parallel lines to a single point on the horizon is clearly illustrated by railroad tracks and telegraph wires, as they vanish in the distance, where earth and sky meet. And as the distance between eye and object increases, the size of the object appears to diminish.

Long Beach
(From the collection of Dr. Ladislas Jaky)
Observation and good composition are perhaps even more vital to a simple theme of this sort than to a very complicated subject. I wanted to suggest the long, barren beach with the lonely cabin, against the sea and the sky. Note how perspective was used to strengthen the composition. I worked with soft pastels on warm gray paper and emphasized the harder objects with bold, dark lines and shadows.

Another valuable aid to learning perspective is intensive study of photographs, especially of architectural subject matter, such as street views and room interiors. Although the camera distorts large objects to some degree, and magnifies items close to the lens, it does give a true general visual image. Try checking your perspective drawing by sketching a subject from actual observation, and then taking a photograph of the subject from the identical viewpoint. Compare the perspective in the two pictures. This practice will help you to develop your sense of perspective very rapidly.

As for color perspective, the first and most important principle to remember is that no color is lighter than white, and no color is darker than black. All colors lie between these two extremes. The darkness or

A square appears square only when seen from direct front center; from any other angle, it assumes a different shape. A circle, too, is a circle only when viewed head-on. All forms change according to your viewpoint, except the sphere, which is exactly the same from every viewpoint.

lightness of any color as compared with black and white is called its *value*. Red, green, blue—each color is easily distinguishable, but each has many different values depending upon the strength of the color and on its distance from the viewer. The thickness of air between an object and the observer is what causes color perspective. The brightest red becomes lighter, somewhat bluish or grayish in tone when seen from a distance. White is not pure white and black is no longer jet black when you look at them from far off. A barren, brownish hill acquires a shade of violet when seen from far off, while a green hill becomes somewhat bluish.

In order to portray an illusion of depth in a color drawing, you must always keep in mind the relative values of all of the colors; that is, the strength of the colors between the two extremes of white and black. If distant objects are rendered in colors as bright and strong as used in near objects, the picture is bound to appear flat and two-dimensional, despite correct linear perspective. Some colors will appear to be jumping out of the picture, while others will resemble holes cut into the paper. In order to achieve realistic three-dimensional color, indicate the very lightest and the very darkest areas first, then relate all the intermediate shades with these two extremes. A gray stone wall in the far distance may be lighter in value than a light blue sky, but the same gray wall appearing in the foreground will be much stronger in value than the sky. Shadows and highlights along the same wall will also differ in value according to their distance from the observer. It is far better to exaggerate the differences than to disregard them. Make the lights even lighter and the darks a little darker to assure sufficient contrast in portraying the true effect of color perspective.

Seashells and Paper

The Green Light

After a heavy snowfall, this Brooklyn street is as Christmasy as any small town. Children play in the snow, cars drive with difficulty, a man in rubber boots clears the sidewalk. I worked on gray paper as a suitable background for the wintry day, darkening the sky color at the horizon. The color of the paper, which shows between white strokes, represents the dirty snow. The title of the painting refers to the traffic signal in front of the bare trees. The green light glows vividly against the dark grays of the picture.

STILL LIFE PAINTING

Landscape, seascape and cityscape subjects all require a certain amount of advance preparation; in addition, each requires some travel and each is dependent, in part, on the whims of the weather. Figure drawing and portraiture may be executed indoors, eliminating the problems of travel and the conditions of climate; however, these depend upon the availability of a model. But there is one inexhaustible source of subject matter at your disposal anywhere, any time. This is the still life.

In town or country, in living room, kitchen or studio, you can set up a still life arrangement and paint it in leisurely comfort. No sudden rain or gust of wind will drive you to shelter; no quickly changing shadows when clouds obscure the sunlight, no unsolicited advice from uninvited spectators. With few exceptions, still life arrangements can be kept over a period of days or weeks, enabling the artist to draw, revise, and complete his pastel in an unhurried fashion, entirely from observation. The exceptions include ripe fruits, quick-fading flowers and other perishables.

The variety of still life subject-matter is endless, and endlessly fascinating. The success of your drawing begins with the care with which you arrange your still life subject. Cézanne, whose apples, oranges and lemons are so famous, spent a great deal of time composing his still-life subjects. He assembled objects of varying sizes, shapes and colors, balancing one against the other—round fruits grouped with an elongated bottle, again a white tablecloth on a rectangular-edged table, all composed in a pleasing asymmetrical pattern. In addition to visual harmony, the objects selected for a still life should have a logical relationship to each other. For example, a vase of flowers, a bowl of fruit and several books might look natural together, and might be found on a library table in any home. If the background of a still life is recognizable, it should have a rational relationship with the foreground objects. Vincent Van Gogh painted a still life of old shoes; set against a background of earth they look perfectly natural. The same shoes, grouped with an arrangement of fruits, flowers and books on a kitchen

56

table, would appear ludicrous, no matter how masterful the painting.

Still life painting affords an endless selection of color combinations, and is eminently suitable subject matter for the pastel artist. No matter how colorful you make your still life set-up, it is wise to include a small white object—a flower, a napkin, a piece of paper—in the composition. The values of other colors are more easily determined when compared with white.

Begin your study with several rough layouts drawn on a small scale in order to perfect the composition. Then do separate studies of the various objects in your set-up in order to learn how to render not only

Composition of Bottles and Jugs
Bottles and jugs come in every conceivable shape and color. Glass bottles are transparent; glazed ceramic jugs are glossy and opaque. Both have bright highlights. Observe carefully the size, shape, color and exact location of each major highlight and shadow. I selected glass and ceramic objects of varied shapes for this study, and found that they looked more realistic when the gray paper showed between strokes

than when, as in the two-handled jug at far left, I spread a solid coat of pastel on the paper. The other objects, done rapidly with just the main darks and lights indicated, seem to sparkle. It is advisable to spray the work before adding final darks and lights. In the case of labels, avoid minute details such as lettering; merely indicate the general size, shape and color of the label, with only a suggestion of outstanding lettering, a trade-mark, or a picture.

58

their shapes and colors but their textural characteristics as well. A peach may resemble an apple in shape, size and coloring; yet there is a great deal of difference between their surface textures. A soft drapery has many folds; the edges of the folds are fluid, rounded, completely unlike the hard, sharp edges in a piece of crumpled paper. In drawing flowers, the anatomical structure of all parts should be carefully scrutinized. Without rendering them photographically, study the number and shape of the petals, the thickness of stem, the size and design of leaf, of every species in your composition.

Most vases are symmetrical. To assure straightness, draw the elliptical mouth of the vase carefully, then draw a vertical line from the center of the mouth to the center of the base. Carefully draw the outline of one side of the vase; then make the other side match by measuring distances from the central line to edge outline at various points.

Select the paper according to the main color effect of your subject. If your set-up contains a large brown table, brown paper will save you a lot of unnecessary background work. Red paper can provide much of the color in a set-up dominated by red drapery. Gray is often a wonderful intermediate color on which bright pastels sparkle while dark tones appear rich and mellow.

Unperishable articles in your still life composition can be painted in a leisurely fashion; but flowers require speed because they wither in hours. Most fruits and vegetables remain paintable for days. Try to finish first the parts that will wither and fade. Compose them carefully in your painting, and later, when the material wilts, you can substitute fresh objects in identical positions. Artificial fruits and flowers can often eliminate the problem of perishable subject matter. Amazingly realistic and inexpensive artificial flowers are now available; when arranged in a vase, they look quite lifelike. With fruits and vegetables, however, only the most expensive imitations create an illusion of reality; the cheaper ones look crude and garish.

Artificial Flowers
Plastic artificial flowers are now made with such perfection that they look quite real, never wilt or die, and can therefore be painted in an unhurried, leisurely fashion. In preparing this still life set-up, I placed a color print, with lots of white paper around it, on the table.

Behind this I placed a vase of artificial flowers; apples, walnuts and a piece of driftwood completed the composition. The rust-colored paper on which I painted provides much of the background and table color. Petals and leaves were painted freely to create a sense of depth and airiness.

Begin to sketch in a neutral color, or outline each object with its own color; for example, sketch a pear with light green, the tablecloth on which it rests with white. Apply the main colors directly. Assume, for example, that you are painting an apple which is half green, half red, with a bright yellow spot. Do not cover the entire outlined shape with red, expecting to add the yellow and green afterward. Green and yellow on top of red would become muddy; a great deal of the pastel would have to be rubbed off. Use each color in its proper place. Employ darker pastels for the shadows; dark finishing lines and bright highlights can be added in the final stages of drawing. If the details are small, as in a bunch of grapes, draw the outlines, rub in the main colors, blend with a fingertip or paper stump, and add the sparkling highlights as the last step, barely touching the paper with the pastel.

Bottles and Jugs, Two Studies
Draw the main shapes and proportions. If you want your bottles and jugs to stand absolutely straight, first draw a vertical line to represent the center of each and sketch the shape evenly on both sides of the line. Draw the mouth, neck, belly and base of each object. Round bottles are symmetrical, but flat ones, especially those with labels or handles, offer problems of perspective. Jugs with handles can be turned one way or another, to achieve more interesting forms.

60

Peaches and Brushes

Step 1. Fresh peaches seemed to be amusing in combination with the glazed jug in which I keep my brushes. I worked on medium-brown paper, almost the color of the table and the wallpaper. I blocked in the subject with light-green pastel, a good neutral color for the items on the table.

Step 2. I applied colors to the peaches, the jug, the folded tablecloth and other portions of the picture, again working all over the paper, rather than finishing one part at a time.

Step 3. Peaches are soft and fuzzy, without strong shadows and lights, while the glazed jug and the metal ferrules of the brushes are hard and shiny. Each must be drawn accordingly to appear in proper relationship with the other. A painting is not finished until the general effect, the dominating characteristic of each object is obtained.

Fish Still Life
Three iridescent fish on a piece of crumpled paper presented a challenging subject. I placed one fish across the others for variety, and counterpointed the smooth, flowing forms with the almost geometric shapes of the wrinkled wrapping paper. Gray charcoal paper proved to be an excellent intermediary color for this subject. I sprayed the work before and after applying the brilliant highlights.

When drawing floral themes, establish the general shape of each flower in the proper color; indicate petals, stems, leaves, dark areas and lights. The color of the background paper is of special significance in a flower still life. It is difficult, tedious and time-consuming to paint the background color around each tiny detail of every flower and leaf. If the color of the paper is in close harmony with the background you are planning to paint, it will not be necessary to fill in background tones close to the outline of each petal, stem and leaf.

Fruits, flowers and vegetables, like all objects, appear different from various angles. A pear's typical pear-shaped outlines are visible only in side view; seen from the top or the bottom, the pear is foreshortened, and round in outline. A rose is round in front view; from the side it is crescent-shaped. Lend variety to your picture by painting your flowers from every conceivable logical angle, as they appear in your still life set-up. Study each item individually, with professional care.

Still life painting first gained prominence as an art theme during the Protestant Reformation, when puritanical Protestants rejected biblical, mythological and historical themes. Obviously, there is little controversial material in still lifes. They are among the most popular pictorial subjects; they are appropriate in almost any room in a house, and compatible with all styles of furnishings. They are also very personal manifestations of the taste and individuality of the artist, since they are assembled by the artist himself, rather than handed down in finished form by nature.

Fruits and Nuts
My aim was to assemble rounded forms—apples, walnuts, jug, glass tray—in a pleasing arrangement, and to balance cool blues with warm yellows and reds. The light-green paper helped to bring out these colors, which were applied with just a few touches of the pastel sticks.

 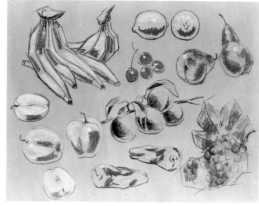

Fruits and Vegetables

Step 1. Sketch the outlines of fruits and vegetables by simplifying them into ovals, circles and other geometric shapes. Do not neglect the main proportions; leave detail work for later.

Step 2. Round out and solidify the geometric forms, using color in fairly flat tones to de-lineate and emphasize shape and depth. Add characteristic details.

Step 3. Apply colors, lights and shadows with more and more definition, until you achieve the desired effect. Draw and paint each item from several angles, and carefully observe the shapes of fruits and vegetables when foreshortened.

Apples and Bananas
This pastel was drawn on dark-brown paper, large portions of which remain untouched in the drapery, the bowl, most of the table, and the shadows on the fruit. I used the pastels flat, but tried to suggest softness in the drapery with cross-hatched lines. A rectangular picture in the background breaks up the curvilinear pattern of the foreground objects.

65

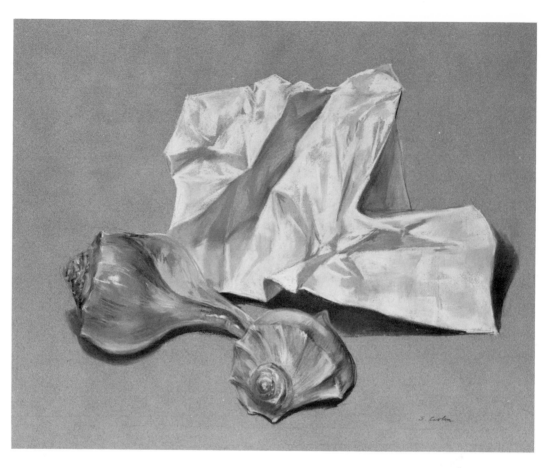

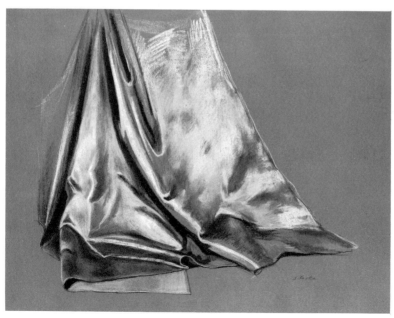

66

TEXTURES

Almost every material has as one of its distinctive characteristics a surface texture; with many materials, this surface texture is so unique that the material can be identified solely through the sense of touch.

Painting is a visual approach. In order to do a realistic rendering of such materials as glass, china, silver, stone, wood, silk, velvet—any material with a texture that is distinguishable and identifiable from a visual as well as a tactile point of view—it is necessary for the artist to observe not only the shape, size and color of the object, but its visual textural characteristics as well.

Chromium, silver and polished steel are readily identifiable without close inspection, because they have certain distinct visual characteristics. They reflect their surroundings in a mirror-like manner; concave or convex shapes in the metal cause distortions in these reflections, which take on a silver-gray tone. Gold and polished brass have similar reflective qualities, but give a golden tint to the images they reflect. Even the clearest wineglass is not invisible; its stem, and the edges of its base and rim are different in color than the bowl of the vessel. Its shape is made visible by the manner in which it distorts and alters the

Seashells and Paper
Shells are hard, and often have sharp ridges and points. Their colors are usually delicate and soft. Paper is brittle, and cracks sharply when folded or crumpled. Lights and shadows are more positively defined on such materials than on pliant, supple silk. Semi-hard pastels are needed for final touches; edges between shaded and illuminated areas are quite harsh. Paper and shells often have a sheen which reflects the colors of the surroundings.

Silk Drapery
Most materials can be recognized from a distance. Silk is one of these, as it has a characteristic soft, shiny appearance. Its folds are rounded; its lights and shadows blend together gradually, but the highlights are crisp and zig-zagged, like lightning. I worked with soft pastels, blending the tones with fingertips and a paper stump, and sprayed the painting before adding a few vivid streaks for highlights.

Spoon in Glass of Water
The transparency of glass can only be rendered by painting objects seen in it or through it. Do not draw a straight spoon in a glass tumbler. Round glass breaks the spoon up visually; water causes further distortion. In this drawing, the spoon appears to be cut into several sections, and appears enlarged at the bottom of the glass. These refractions and distortions must be carefully noted, and precisely rendered, in order to produce a realistic drawing. Even when a glass is colorless, shadows and highlights are clearly visible. Work on grayish or greenish paper, and employ white pastel pencil for highlights.

Fur Scarf
For a study such as this, work on a colored paper that will bring out the tones of the fur. Use sharp-pointed, semi-hard sticks, or pastel pencils. Don't attempt to draw every hair of the fur; study the way the hairs grow from the skin; observe their length, direction, color. Normally, the tip of the hair is lighter than the root. Do not expect to obtain the appearance of fur simply by smudging the paper; you must show the hairy texture of the material.

68

Glass Vase with Iris
Although water and glass are colorless, lights and shadows keep them from being invisible. In a vase of flowers, the stems, under water, are refracted, broken up. A colored glass changes the colors as well as the shapes of objects in or behind it. A blue object seen through a red glass appears to be violet; the same object seen through yellow glass looks green.

appearance of objects seen through it, and in the shapes and locations of highlights on its surface.

Textiles are dull-finished, or very shiny, or somewhere between these two extremes. Fruits and vegetables may be fuzzy, glossy, coarse, wrinkled, smooth, dull. With close observation and practice, each of these textures can be rendered realistically, in an easily identifiable manner.

Fuzzy objects can be drawn with the tip of the pastel in dots, short or long lines in parallel or crosshatched strokes; experimentation will lead you to the desired effect. For glossy textures, rub the basic colors into the paper with fingertips or a tissue, then apply sharp, contrasting shadows and bright highlights. One successful technique involves spraying the nearly completed pastel with a fixative before applying the darkest and brightest strokes. Observe all shadows and lights closely. No matter how dark a shadow may be, it is never jet-black, but is dominated by a dark value of a color, perhaps blue, purple, or brown,

69

only close inspection will tell you. Highlights are seldom pure white. When seen on glossy, reflective surfaces, they are often tiny images of the source of light, the window, or the lamp, greatly reduced in size and more or less distorted by the shape of the article in which they are reflected.

Glassware is normally transparent, but only a flawless piece of flat glass leaves objects seen through it unchanged in size and form. In all cases, colors are somewhat softened when seen through glass. Here is a study devised to help you to understand how to render glass realistically.

Violin and Old Books
The violin is difficult to draw, but its distinguished beauty is worth the effort. I placed the instrument on old, leather-bound books, on maroon velvet. The white paper placed beneath the instrument enlivens the others colors. Several textures were involved: the glossy violin with its smooth, yellowish highlights, the velvet with softly blended tones, and the crisp paper.

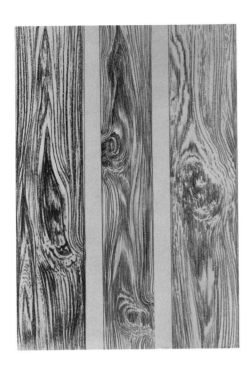

Wood Planks

The appearance of wood is determined by several factors: species, age, exposure to weather. However, the most significant characteristic, and the one demanding closest scrutiny, is grain. It is not enough to draw wavy lines and curlicues; the design of a plank's graining is organic, and requires careful observation if a realistic rendering is to be produced. I drew three planks on buff paper in dark, semi-hard pastels, studying lines and knots.

Tree Bark

In landscape painting, the main pattern and color of the bark of trees should be observed and followed, even though minute details be omitted. In order to study the characteristics of tree bark, I prepared a still life composition of three pieces of split logs. The picture was drawn on dark-green paper with soft pastels.

Place a teaspoon in a half-filled water glass. You will notice that the spoon appears to be broken in several places; it also appears greatly enlarged at the bottom of the glass. The table and tablecloth also seem to be broken, shifted, slightly melted when seen through the glass. All these facts must be indicated in your painting. Water, too, may seem colorless in small quantities, in a glass for instance, but great quantities of water, such as in a lake or river, are constantly taking on new tones. Reflections in water are clear if the water is calm, rough if its surface is rippled by a passing breeze, broken up into hundreds of lights and shadows by turbulent waves. In mirrors and vertical planes of metal, reflected images are reversed from right to left; in water, reflections are reversed from top to bottom, as they would be in a mirror

71

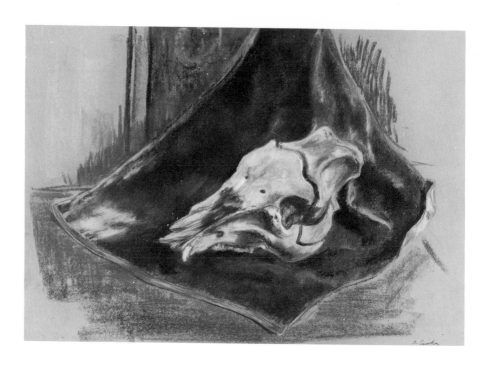

Skull on Velvet

The contrast of the hard yellow-white skull against the soft dark-red velvet presented a challenge. I worked on light-brown paper, so that I could leave much of the background untouched. I used soft pastels and sprayed the picture before switching to semi-hard sticks to define the shadows and crevices of the skull with dark-brown and burnt sienna lines, made with semi-hard sticks.

placed on the floor. The relative position and size of an object so reflected are the same as the object itself. Your image is life-size if you stand close to a mirror; the reflection diminishes as you step away from the mirror. The inverted image of a house reflected in a lake always appears directly below the house itself. A distant object is just as much smaller in the reflection as in the actual scene being reflected. You can paint a mirror, or a lake, by painting the image reflected in it.

There is no special difficulty in rendering textures beyond training your powers of observation, and learning to reproduce accurately the things you observe. Make studies of individual items before you begin to paint a large pastel in which these materials and textures will appear. It is interesting to note that the most modern abstract artists—Matisse and Braque among others—pay a great deal of attention to textural variations, even when they completely disregard realistic details in other respects. Textural variety lends richness to practically any painting, whatever its style, however abstract or representational its approach.

72

THE FIGURE

Figure painting is a highly admired and respected art form among professional artists. Anyone who has attempted drawing the human figure from life is aware of the difficulties involved. One problem confronting the figure painter is that the human figure, even in repose, is never absolutely still. Each anatomical portion of the human form is exceedingly complex; an apple is pretty much the same shape from any angle, but a hand can assume a great variety of shapes, each one complicated and demanding of close observation and precise drawing. Another difficulty lies in the fact that while no two humans are exactly alike, there is so much basic similarity between their forms that any error in the artist's representation will be obvious. Who will notice if you paint a branch of a tree bigger than it actually is? But if you paint a human leg too short, a head too large, your work will appear distorted and grotesque.

Subject matter has nothing to do with artistry. Esthetically, it makes no difference whether you paint fruits or figures. The only difference lies in the nature of figure drawing, and its demand for keen observation and precise draftsmanship. Do not allow this to frighten you. You can learn to paint figures as you can learn to paint any other subject. A knowledge of anatomy, while helpful, is not imperative. The ancient Greeks' mastery of anatomy in art resulted from their ability to observe the human body, to notice, measure and render every detail; from their observation, they selected a set of perfect, ideal proportions as a permanent standard.

Although it is practically impossible to create finished, representational figure paintings without life models, it is advisable to augment sketching from life with study of the general construction and proportions of the human body by drawing from plaster-casts or from manikins. Good casts are expensive, fragile, and too bulky to store comfortably in most homes. Manikins are ingeniously constructed to duplicate the anatomical actions and limitations of human bones and joints; each section can be turned and twisted to the same extent as the corresponding part of the living body, so that every position the human body can assume can be duplicated by manipulating the joints of the manikin. The manikin is constructed in perfect proportions— a great aid to the art student, who can study the correct proportions of the human body simply by measuring parts of the manikin in relation to each other. A good 15″ or 18″ manikin is a wise investment for the experienced artist as well as for the art student.

When you work from a manikin, try to visualize it as a human model made of flesh, bone and muscle, rather than wood and wire. Consider each mechanical joint as an articulation of two bones. Emphasize motion and proportions; manipulate the manikin in standing, walking, sitting, running, dancing, fighting, leaning, reclining positions; study and sketch your model from every conceivable angle. Quick sketches made with the tip of the pastel, without any shading or blending, are particularly valuable preparation for later, more complete studies after you have become thoroughly familiar with the visual intricacies of the human figure.

For an entirely different, but equally valuable exercise, carry a small sketchbook wherever you go, for recording spontaneous sketches of unposed human figures. On a bus, in a restaurant, in the park, pick your subject and try to sketch him quickly, unobtrusively, so that he is not aware of what you are doing. These spontaneous studies are of immense benefit to the artist in studying the human form.

In figures even more than in other subjects, take a good look at the main forms, rather than at the tiny details. Observe the general direction of an arm, a leg or the torso. Simplify each portion of the figure into the geometric shape it most closely resembles; reduce the skeletal structure to a series of sticks. It is simple to make a good drawing by observing these geometric forms and by sketching stick figures, in which only the direction and comparative size of each part of the body are shown with a line, or a simple solid form. The position of the legs is of special importance. Is the model supporting his weight evenly on both legs, or leaning more heavily on one? How much space is there between the feet? What is the direction of each thigh and leg in relationship to the vertical and the horizontal? Indicate these directions with straight lines before beginning to model the leg in detail.

Photographs, magazine illustrations and art reproductions will also help you toward an understanding of the human body. The great

Beach Scene

This painting was done on rough watercolor paper. I first applied a watercolor wash in brown on the lower half of the sheet, and in bright blue on the upper half, in order to represent the beach and the sky. This eliminated the need to apply a background in pastels—a tedious, time-consuming job in view of the complicated figures in the foreground. I drew the dark outlines quickly then added the most important colors in soft pastels. My intent was to capture the rapid forward movement of a group of men, women and children rushing into the surf.

Figure Sketches

Practice in figure sketching is essential for learning to reproduce the human form in a factual, realistic manner. Whether these sketches are made from life, or from adjustable artists' manikins, they help you to study the proportions of the figure, and the postures it is capable of assuming—preliminary lessons basic to the rendering of the finished figure.

masters of the past often found inspiration and aid in the work of other, often lesser artists, long before the advent of the camera.

Needless to say, the most valuable lessons in the study of the human body are to be learned in working from professional life models. Sketching from nude models is a time-tested tradition in the art of western civilization. It enables the artist to observe the complete body, and to understand its actions. Certain costumed figures, such as models posed in dancing outfits or swimsuits, are just as valuable as subjects for life sketches, provided the costumes do not obscure the anatomical structure of the figures.

Sketch groups are often organized by artists and students, with each participant paying his share of the expenses. Join such a group if you have the opportunity; it will enable you to have periodical sessions of life study for a fairly reasonable price.

Hands

Hands, properly drawn, can be very expressive elements of a finished figure drawing; they merit considerable sketching practice. Draw your own hands from different angles, beginning with outlines in a somewhat geometric form, before going into detailed study.

Feet

Draw feet from as many angles as possible, in repose and in action. Approach the subject as you approach the problem of sketching hands, beginning with basic shape and proportions, then developing details.

Two Ballerinas

This drawing began as a five-minute sketch. For a two-figure sketch such as this, you need only one model. Draw her in one pose, then in another, alongside the first drawing. In developing this drawing, executed in red pastel, I emphasized graceful movements, suggesting forms by sketching in main shadows, without further elaboration.

78

The most important principle to remember in life drawing is to work from large to small. Concentrate on the pose, the proportion, the main action of the figure. Study the position of the head, the neck and the shoulders in relation to each other. Study the model from a number of different locations in the room, before beginning to sketch. The posed figure can be observed from many angles and locations; the same pose is altered radically each time the observer moves. Notice the twisting of the body, the foreshortening of arms and legs, especially in sitting or reclining postures. It is not difficult to render a foreshortened view if you are sufficiently observant.

As soon as you have established the correct proportions and gestures, indicate the figure in the proper flesh-tones. Add details with semi-hard pastels, gradually. Pastel pencils are ideal for pure line drawing in which no shading is contemplated. These line drawings require skill, but they are worth the trouble since this delicate line work will ultimately be necessary for the finishing of a figure painting.

Three Ballerinas
Employing the same model again in various poses, I composed my picture carefully, and added dashes of realistic color.

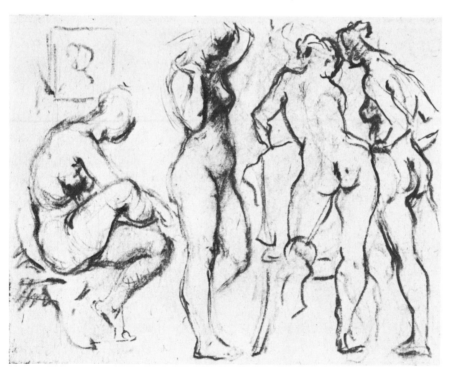

Five-Minute Sketches

Rapid figure-sketching helps you to develop the ability to observe general forms and proportions; a five-minute figure sketch just doesn't allow time for details as well. Learn to draw the entire figure at one time—head, shoulders, torso, arms, legs—rather than working on each separately. Begin with stick-figures; concentrate first on proportions and poses. Then develop the shape and form of the body, omitting details.

In addition to sketching the entire figure, study various parts of it in more minute detail, on a larger scale, in life-size if possible. Sketch your own hands and feet; ask your friends to permit you to do quick studies of them, concentrating on feet, knees, elbows, arms, until you are thoroughly familiar with the anatomical construction of the human figure. Whatever anatomical part you may study, first observe its general shape and proportions. If you begin a sketch of a hand by drawing the thumbnail first, and then proceed, working in detail, with the rest of the fingers, your sketch will very likely be distorted and out of proportion.

Make studies of apparel, too, particularly shoes, hats and gloves, which have the same foreshortened views that feet, heads and hands have. Since most of your models will be clothed, it is absolutely necessary for you to scrutinize the clothing they will wear. A coat, a skirt, a woman's pocketbook or a man's attaché case must be rendered as realistically as the figures wearing them, for successful figure compositions.

THE FINISHED FIGURE: In the past, a painting was considered finished only after the artist had painted every portion of it to perfection. This is still true of the school of *magic realist* art, but most present-day representational artists settle for some point between the two extremes of microscopic detail and almost featureless *impressionism*. To all intents and purposes, a work is finished when the artist himself is satisfied with the results he has achieved. First, you must know what it is you want to achieve—what objective you are trying to attain. Your subject often predetermines the degree to which a painting should be finished. A quiet figure, sitting, reading or sleeping, should be rendered with more detail than a figure caught in action, such as a ballerina in the midst of a pirouette, or an athlete clearing a hurdle. A more detailed work suggests rest, while a somewhat blurred image implies motion and speed.

In my sketches of dancers, I attempted to show movement. I emphasized action, forms, breezy tulle skirts, the muscular, well-formed legs of the ballet dancers. Facial features, hands, hair, fingers, shoe ribbons are indicated with a few strokes, since it is not possible to observe these details on rapidly moving dancers. Three dimensional form and spatial relationships between figures and backdrops were emphasized to heighten the drama of the theatrical setting.

In drawing figure subjects, the proportions, careful balancing of each

Standing Nude

The human flesh is not the same tone all over the body; observe the subtle differences, in order to make your nude studies more realistic. Usually, the skin tones are yellowish on the back; the arms and lower legs are pinkish or slightly violet, and the thighs have a greenish tint. For this study, I worked on an even-grain white drawing paper with flat pieces of pastels. I made the outlines very heavy and dark, in soft pastels, to bring out the solidity of the female figure.

82

Resting Dancers

Step. 1. After several preliminary sketches, I drew these figures on rust-colored paper.

Step. 2 Carried to a higher degree of execution, the picture is still sketchy, yet satisfactory from an artistic point of view. Such figures would look stiff and static if they were finished in photographic detail.

figure, and correct rendering of foreshortened limbs are of utmost significance. Whether you paint a single person or a group, in repose or in action, make several sketches before attempting a finished painting. When you have achieved a composition that pleases you, draw it in pencil on a sheet of tracing paper, in full scale. Make a carbon of your drawing by covering the back of the tracing paper with pastel of any color that will stand out well against the color of the paper you have selected for your final drawing. Place the tracing over your drawing paper, fastening the two together with masking tape at the corners, to keep the tracing from slipping and smudging the drawing paper. Now go over your tracing with a hard red or green pencil. The color is necessary in order to indicate which parts of the drawing have already been traced. Press the colored pencil hard enough and the lines will be transferred clearly in pastel on your drawing paper. You thus eliminate much changing and erasing on your good paper.

Start applying the colors directly. Remember that the characteristic brilliance for which pastels are justifiably famous disappears after too many erasures and corrections. It is not possible to avoid erasures by piling on layer after layer of pastel indefinitely; even the strongest paper cannot take this kind of punishment. The best results are achieved with a single application of pastels, with the inevitable addition of shading and highlights. The finishing touches should be applied with semi-hard pastels sharpened to a point, or even better, with pastel pencils.

It is most helpful to work on a paper the color of which suits the background of your subject. In this way you can avoid the troublesome necessity of working your background tones close to every delicate outline of the main forms. Values are more important to successful figure painting than to work with other subject matter, because the loveliness of human flesh-tones is quickly destroyed by shadows that are too dark, highlights that are too bright. Compare the value of a shadow on the human flesh with that of a shadow on a dark carpet, and you will realize that the darkest spot on the body is lighter than the brightest spot on the carpet. Note the fine shades of he skin, the many different tones. There is no single flesh color which can be spread all over the drawing of a human figure, like a coat of paint. The lower arms are often pink, the upper arms yellowish; the lower legs are violet- or pink-tinted. Give your figure drawings life and artistry by observing the finer nuances. Painting implies the use of colors; train your eyes to see all of them, not just a few basic ones.

BABIES

It is a well-known fact that babies and little children are inactive only while they are asleep. Great patience is required when using children as subjects, even for candid photography. Sketching babies is unquestionably nerve-racking, but it is an intriguing and rewarding experience as well. Children are not just small adults. Their proportions differ considerably from those of grown-ups. The head of a baby is relatively large, so are its eyes. The nose and mouth, on the other hand, are tiny. The cheeks are round, the forehead bulging. Arms, legs and body are plump; joints are defined by wrinkles.

Sketching a sleeping baby is simple enough, but you miss the beauty of its big, shiny eyes, its expression of awareness. Try to sketch babies by beginning a new drawing each time the baby moves; continue these sketches whenever the child resumes one of the original positions. Make several drawings on a single sheet of paper. As each position which the baby can possibly assume is bound to be repeated again and again, you will eventually achieve a set of complete sketches. The same procedure is recommended for sketching all fast-moving subjects.

Photography is almost indispensable in the study of baby portraiture. The camera is capable of creating a complete image in a fraction of a second. By taking many pictures, you can study proportions, gestures, facial expressions of your tiny subjects. After you have obtained a satisfactory photograph, make a detailed drawing of it on a sheet of good pastel or charcoal paper; then proceed as usual, observing and applying the colors. Once the proportions are properly established, colors present no problems. Little children have soft, undeveloped, changeable features; avoid precisely defined, hard lines which might make a child appear prematurely old. The eye cavities are visible in the face of a baby, but there are no pockets under the eyes, as in the case of a mature person. The nostrils are soft and rounded; there are no sharp lines connecting them with the corners of the mouth.

Jamie Coloring a Book
A child is much more easily observed, and sketched, when engrossed in some absorbing work, than when moving about. I recorded the main forms and colors of this drawing before Jamie even noticed what I was doing. I worked in full color on ochre paper.

The Baby
These sketches were drawn rapidly in red pastel on cream paper. It may be necessary to make a dozen or more drawings before obtaining a satisfactory one, but the subject warrants the effort if the baby is close to your heart.

Head of Jamie
These four views were sketched while the little
girl was busy coloring a picture book. Each
time she changed position, I began another
sketch.

The head of a new-born baby comprises one-fourth of the length of
its entire body. As the baby matures, the body grows more rapidly
than the head. The proportions change to one-fifth, then one-sixth,
until the head constitutes slightly less than one-seventh the total height
of a fully grown being. The skull's proportions and shape change, too.
The face becomes longer; the distance between the eyes and the nostrils
increases; the forehead ceases to bulge out; the cheeks lose their peach-
like plumpness, and the cheek-bones and jaws become more clearly
defined. Muscles and bones lengthen, taking up the slack in the skin.
This gradual development requires close observation for understanding
and mastery, essential for producing convincing pictures of babies and
children.

Painting likenesses of babies and children is a specialized field, one
in which the artist can be successful only if he loves children and knows
instinctively how to handle them. Then, painting children can be an
enjoyable hobby, and a lucrative profession as well.

88

PAINTING THE HEAD

Throughout the ages, people have surrounded themselves with images of beloved or important persons for magical, religious or sentimental reasons. In prehistoric times, such images were hardly more than crude symbols. In more advanced communities, however, a great deal of skill was developed in creating these early portraits. The ancient Egyptians believed that eternal life after death was dependent upon the existence of the mummified body, or at least an exact likeness, of the deceased. As a result, the faces of their statues and paintings became more and more realistic. Portraiture reached a level of unsurpassed magnificence in the time of the Roman Empire, due to ancestor worship, for which

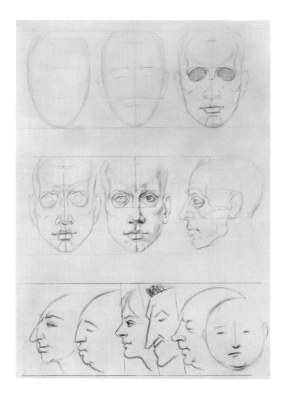

Head Studies
The very first step in learning to draw the human head is to sketch very simply, blocking in the general proportions, indicating eyebrows, tip of nose and location of mouth with a few lines. Draw an outline of the head, then add a center line for the nose; suggest the eye cavities, omitting other details. Whether you draw full face or profile views, proportions are more essential than delicate details.

89

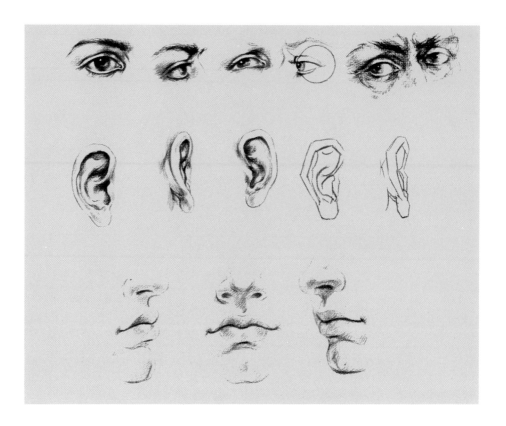

Details of the Head

Study the eyes, nose and mouth from various angles. Draw them individually first, then in proper proportion and location in a simple head study. The foreshortening of every detail is significant. If the head is seen from above, the nose, mouth and eyes are seen from the same viewpoint.

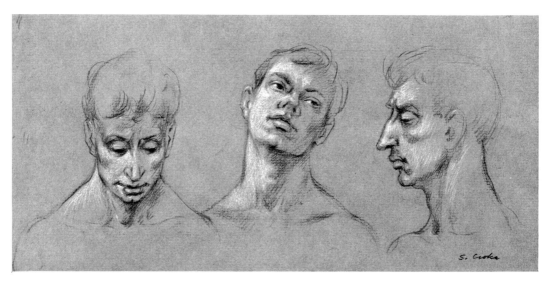

Three Heads
In these studies, I was interested primarily in capturing various facial expressions. The eyes and the mouth are the most expressive features; learn to draw them well in order to give your portrait studies character.

perfect portraits of the deceased were required.

The human face, with its endless variety of features, expressions and moods, is a fascinating subject from a purely artistic viewpoint. Although photography may at present satisfy the average person's desire for likenesses, portraits painted by artists are as highly prized as ever.

Before you can paint portraits bearing a reasonable likeness of the subject, you must develop the ability to draw heads in general. All heads have the same anatomical construction, despite the differences of features which enable us to recognize and identify individuals. Most heads are round or oval in shape; however, very narrow, and somewhat pear-shaped heads are not uncommon, either. For the sake of determining accurate proportions, the face can be divided into three sections: from the top of the head to the eyebrows, from the eyebrows to the bottom of the nose, and from nose to bottom of chin. In the idealized proportions of ancient Greek art, these three sections were of identical size. The two sides of the face are symmetrical, but never exactly alike. Eyes can be close-set or far-set; noses come in a wide variety of sizes and shapes; the lower lip is usually thicker than the upper lip, and the mouth can be very large or very small, set close beneath the nose, or close to the chin. The chin may be square, round, pointed, protruding or receding, small or large. The ears, often neglected by inexperienced artists, are just as characteristic and individual as the rest of the features.

91

Helmeted Soldiers

To lend variety to your portrait studies, try
working from a costume model. If you have no
picturesque old hats, coats or gowns, you can
rent these from theatrical or masquerade costume dealers. For the costume portrait shown
here, I wanted to depict strong-featured, rough-
looking Roman legionnaires. I worked on yellow paper, appropriate to both the skin tones
and the golden helmets. For a study of this sort,
in which power and strength predominate,
forceful contrasts of lights and shadows are
more effective than smooth blending.

Double Self-Portrait

The three-quarter view was drawn first, from a
mirror set to one side. Then I set up a second
mirror, which reflected my profile into the
first mirror. This sounds tricky, but is really
quite simple, requiring only two clear mirrors
and a place to stand or hang them in the proper
positions.

Self-Portrait

This serious, complete study was drawn with the aid of a mirror. I began with general outlines, then added more and more detail in order to achieve true resemblance. I rubbed the tones into the buff velvet paper with my fingertips. Eyelids and nostrils were drawn with pastel pencils, blended first with a fine stump and then with a small brush. Whenever excessive pastel accumulated on the paper, I removed it with a bristle brush before continuing with the drawing.

A common mistake made by students is to draw the eye with two pointed corners, placing a small disk in the center for the iris. Actually, the eye has a rounded tear duct in the inner corner next to the nose; the outer corner is pointed, where the upper eyelid overlaps the lower one. The iris is round, but its upper third is generally covered by the eyelid, except when the eyes stare in fright or surprise, and appear to be popping out. The eyelashes on the upper lid are longer and denser than those on the lower lid.

When sketching the head, concentrate first on the outlines, the position of the eyebrows, the tip of the nose, the placement of the mouth. Next, indicate the irises, then a suggestion of the nostrils and the division between upper and lower lips. Once you have established these features, correct the outlines of the face, add the ears if you see them, the hair on the temples and the forehead, and draw the neck. Now begin to model the eyelids, simple shaded areas on the side of the nose, along the chin, on the sides of the cheeks, working on the whole head at once, not just one small portion at a time. Use a semi-hard dark pastel for the basic sketch, soft pastels for flesh-tones and shadows. The finishing touches can best be done in pastel pencils.

Using the same model and the identical pose, make several sketches in the same scale, side by side on the same sheet of paper, of full-face, profile and three-quarter views. Then compare the corresponding features of each sketch. From the front, the eyes and mouth are most prominent; in profile, the nose and chin are the most characteristic forms. The three-quarter view is perhaps the most popular because it shows more of the character of the face than either of the other views. As the head turns, you see more and more of one side, and correspondingly less of the other side. Each feature changes, also, as the head turns away. In order to render a realistic head, you must train yourself to observe and record these changes accurately.

An excellent way to study the head is by sketching from plaster-casts. Details are easily observed in casts, since they do not move, as live models do. Sketching from photographs is also a good way to develop an understanding of the foreshortening which occurs as the human head is observed from various angles. Self-portraiture, with the aid of a mirror, is excellent practice, too, with the added advantage that your model is always available. A full-face or three-quarter view is easy to manage; a self-portrait in profile requires two mirrors, a much more complicated procedure.

Whatever head you choose for your subject, draw it with care, from

94

Girl with Cigarette

Her pensive mood inspired me to make a life-size sketch of this model. The relaxed pose, with elbows resting on the table, arms folded, cigar-ette dangling from her fingertips, adds interest and atmosphere to the picture, drawn with black pastel pencil on buff paper.

observation, rather than from memory. Resist the temptation to exaggerate; this can quickly turn a serious portrait study into a caricature. Try working in life-size, at first, so you can take measurements of your subject to avoid or correct major proportional errors. You might try doing a portrait drawing, and then taking a photograph of the model from the same angle; have the photograph enlarged photostatically to the size of your painting and compare the two. The comparison may shock you a bit, but will be of tremendous assistance to you in future work.

For portrait painting in pastels, the paper should be of a color that harmonizes with the middle tones of the head. A soft gray paper lends itself to the rendering of a delicately pale subject; buff or light brown is a good choice when the sitter has a darker, ruddier skin. For a soft, youthful head, rub the pastel into the paper; blend shadows and lights with your fingertip or a paper stump. Older, more powerful faces should be represented in bolder strokes, expressive of character and strength.

Select your color values carefully in portrait work; beware of painting the shadows black or dark purple and the highlights pure white. In the human face, only the pupils of the eyes can be considered black. Only the highlights on a white object, such as a dress or shirt, can be pure white. A shadow painted too dark looks like a hole in the face; a big white highlight creates the impression of a piece of white paper accidentally stuck to the painting. After establishing all main forms and colors, render the fine details with semi-hard pastel sticks or pastel pencils. A light spraying of fixative before completion enables you to apply the brightest highlights and the finest shadows with precision, and without fear of smudging your work.

CHARACTER HEADS: Older faces are marked by strongly developed features, deep lines and shadows, and often a more pronounced skeletal structure than can be observed in younger people. Occasionally, a more mature person has such pronounced features and facial expression that his head makes a good character study. If you have an opportunity to paint such a subject realistically, without the slightest flattery, you can learn a great deal about portraiture. Avoid exaggeration of queer or distorted facial characteristics; render them honestly, neither stressing nor understating them. It would never occur to me to paint a freak, or a misshapen person; this would be cruel. But a face that reflects suffering, intelligence, determination, a sense of humor, is an inspiration to any artist interested in people in general and human physiognomy in particular.

Likeness is much simpler to achieve in character studies than in portraits of younger, less individualized heads. Avoid distortions that might be insulting to the model, but do not flatter dishonestly. Sketch the features, and apply the colors as in ordinary portrait work, but keep blending to a minimum. The anatomy of the oldest face is similar to that of the loveliest; the difference lies in the development of some, or perhaps all of the features. In the mature face, one feature is often particularly prominent, dominating the entire appearance. Carefully rendered characteristics—a moustache, beard, bushy eyebrows, piercing eyes, pensive mouth—add to the power of a character head. Some of the artists specializing in slick society portraits paint character studies as a welcome relief from the idealized, flattering pictures which they produce for a livelihood.

Redhead
The subject of this drawing has a strong-featured, plump face, a staring eye, and a protruding lower lip beneath a mouth which appears to be fixed in a slightly open position.

These characteristics were exaggerated in the drawing for the sake of emphasis. Light-gray paper sets off the red hair and the ochre flesh tones.

Study of a Woman's Head
This is a purely artistic picture of an attractive young woman, drawn with soft tones on brownish-gray board. The features are suggested, rather than completely defined; character has not been concealed.

Screaming Girl

In a character study, beauty is of no concern to the artist. He is fascinated by strong or unusual features and expressions. A little exaggeration or distortion can be helpful in emphasizing expression or depicting emotion in character portraiture. In this study, I wanted to capture the terrified expression, the loud scream. Eyelashes and other minute facial details were omitted; I concentrated on the bulging eyes and wide-open mouth, in order to achieve the expression of fear.

Uncle George
Step 1. An elderly man with a long nose, wide mouth, and strongly defined bone structure is easier to render than a beautiful young girl. As with all portrait work, the outlines and main

colors precede detail work.
Step 2. Logical and gradual development, adding form and color to a well-established sketch, eliminates the need for extensive changing and correcting.

Uncle George
The finished portrait is the result of acute observation of proportions, shapes, colors, lights and shadows. I worked on yellow-ochre paper with pointed semi-hard pastels for linear work, soft pastels for face, hair and garment. In drawing character portraits such as this, avoid exaggeration, or your portrait will become a caricature. Flesh tones change from one portion of

the face to another; temples, forehead, ears, nose, chin, cheeks are all noticeably different in color. The shadows and highlights cast on flesh tones are not merely darker or lighter shades of the same color, but are reflections of the surroundings as well, and may be brownish, greenish, yellowish, bluish in accordance with the colors of the background and setting.

Phantom Riders

I began this abstract drawing with a perfectly realistic sketch of a horse, drawn in brown pastel on buff, sanded paper. Then I distorted the head, neck, body and legs in order to emphasize the rearing posture, and added suggestions of human figures with bold strokes of flat pastels. Burnt sienna and purple predominate over smaller areas of yellow and light blue.

ABSTRACTION

Traditionally trained artists and untutored laymen are often disturbed by the word "abstraction." They think of it as a radical new concept; yet abstract art dates back to the prehistoric cave painter. The artists of the Aztec and Mayan civilizations abstracted human and animal forms to produce wonderfully decorative designs for textiles, carvings and pottery. The discovery of African art during the Anglo-Boer War (1899-1902) had tremendous impact on the art of the West. Its deliberately distorted, exaggerated, dehumanized statues met the needs of western artists in their endless search for new forms of expression. Abstraction was a logical sequel to impressionism and cubism.

Abstraction, in a brief definition, means the simplification of objects to basic forms and colors. In other words, it is an elimination of superficial ornaments and details. A true abstraction is recognizable because it contains identifiable elements of reality. Contrary to popular opinion, it is not work that a child can produce. A serious abstractionist replaces lifelike details with careful organization of colors, shapes and textures. A comparison of the lines and forms in a fine abstraction with the lines and forms of a perfectly realistic painting of the same subject will reveal a startling relationship between the two. Despite their vastly different appearances, they share similar pictorial qualities and techniques.

Most present-day representational artists lay out their preliminary sketches as if they were preparing to paint abstractions, indicating with simple lines and forms the position, size, shape and color of each important element in the painting. The representational artist continues to work over this layout until it becomes realistically complete. The abstractionist concentrates on making the original pattern more solid, more definite, enriched in color and textural effects. An abstraction can be flat or three-dimensional in appearance, depending upon the artist's desired effect; it can be loosely, freely painted, or very precisely,

Autumn Rhapsody
My aim was not to depict a realistic scene, but
to render the brilliant color combinations so
characteristic of the autumn season. The yellow,
orange, gold, rust, red, and lavender tones
literally glow against the sparkling blue of the
clear sky. This is a true abstraction. Trees are
barely suggested with a few strokes. I wanted
the colors to sing.

Prodigal Son
Working on brown paper, I drew directly in
strong, unrealistic colors, without any blending.
In this semi-abstract painting, the design is of
primary importance; the narrow vertical shape
of the drawing strengthens the composition and
heightens its emotional content.

Consolation

Two persons, united in sorrow, are painted in a composition that intensifies the impact of their grief. Arms and bodies are wrapped together in a closely knit, unified design. Every portion of the painting is simplified and stylized; emotional impact takes precedence over realism.

Mother and Child

Here, too, the pattern is abstract, but the subject can easily be seen. It is not necessary to make abstractions of completely unrecognizable elements. In this drawing, I wished to evoke a mood, a sentiment. I worked on light-green paper with a few powerful colors and dark, swinging, spiraling lines.

carefully executed. We speak of abstract and semi-abstract works, depending upon the extent to which the artist has departed from realistic representation.

Proponents of abstract art have been known to comment, on viewing a fine realistic painting: "If only the artist had stopped when his composition was laid out, he'd have a masterpiece." Traditional painters, on the other hand, might just as logically criticize an attractive abstraction by saying, "The composition is beautiful; too bad the artist did not develop it into a realistic painting." There is plenty of room for both points of view; posterity will be the final judge.

Whatever his ultimate preference, every student of art should try working in an abstract way, in order to learn how to eliminate superfluous details. These details usually interfere with sound composition and brilliant execution. Abstract painting is not to be confused with non-objective, automatic or abstract-expressionist art; these schools claim to be devoid of any connection with reality.

There are two basic approaches to the execution of an abstract painting. In the first approach, only the main forms of a subject are sketched in flat, two-dimensional pattern, closely resembling a patchwork quilt consisting of swatches of various shapes and colors. The second method begins with a fairly realistic layout; then the artist reduces each object to its simplest form. The first method is a direct approach, the second is indirect; the final results are often quite similar.

Abstractions can be most decorative; they can have intricate patterns and beautiful color-combinations. An abstract stained-glass window may be as inspired and magnificent as one filled with biblical figures and pictorial subject matter. There is, however, one difficulty, abstract art cannot be judged as easily as traditional, representational work, because it has no realistic details and proportions. Errors in a realistic work can be detected by an observant layman. But critical comment can be summarily dismissed by the abstract artist with the blunt statement: "This is just the way I wanted to paint my picture. Any camera can do a realistic job!"

Although it is my conviction that some of the greatest art works produced in the twentieth century are abstractions, I also believe that an artist must first learn to draw and paint realistically, correctly, before he can paint successful abstractions. In other words, abstraction should be a gradual development in art, not a shortcut to flashy, superficial effects.

A PORTFOLIO OF SKETCHES

Sketching is as important to the development of the artist as finger exercises are to the skill of the concert pianist. Finger exercises are not works of art in themselves, but sketches can possess real artistic value. A quick, spontaneous sketch may one day be the inspiration and the reference source for an important, serious painting.

Parks and the zoos are among the best sources for sketch material. Only larger cities possess zoological gardens of any size, but every town has some sort of park. The principles of sketching remain the same regardless of subject matter, but parks and zoos offer more fun, more problems, and greater esthetic rewards than most other locations, due to the endless variety inherent to the subject matter found there.

A photograph can be snapped quickly, but the result is always a "still," a picture lacking the animation of the actual scene. A sketch produces results that are much more satisfactory, since it can represent not only the subject, but the action, the motion of the subject, as well. Before attempting to sketch, study your subject carefully; follow the movements of humans, or animals for a while, in order to become acquainted with their rhythms. Such subjects have great variety in action, and their actions are repeated. The Impressionists discovered a method of rendering this busy restlessness. They omitted small details, concentrating on essential gestures, forms and colors, thus creating an impression of incessant motion. Pastels are an ideal medium for rendering motion, since they can be applied rapidly; even the nature of the stroke can give the impression of speed and action.

Photography, with all its limitations, can be very helpful to the art student attempting to draw animals for the first time. The snapshot can record proportions and features of unfamiliar animals; these can be studied at leisure, away from the source of the subject matter. Use photographs for studying and understanding unfamiliar details, such as the shape of an animal's nostrils, ears, legs and hooves. These features are difficult to absorb from on-the-spot observation of an animal in motion, but can be frozen on film for reference at another time and place.

The sketching of animals in motion should be approached in the same way as the sketching of babies. Draw one sketch after another on the same sheet of paper, beginning a new sketch every time the animal changes position, and returning to previous sketches each time the animal resumes a position previously drawn. Some of your sketches are bound to be good, but regardless of the appearance of the finished product, you will enjoy the exhilaration of rapid sketching and you

will learn a great deal. If you learn to sketch figures in motion, it will be that much easier for you to sketch them in repose.

Animals, like babies, will occasionally remain still. Try to work in more detail on these occasions. Sleeping animals are extremely charming, and make delightful subjects for sketches. The grizzliest bear and the most ferocious lion resemble gentle babies when sound asleep. Most modern zoos attempt to recreate the animals' natural habitats within their compounds. Try to include some indications of background in your animal sketches, to enhance the effect of reality.

Some parks are formal and artificial, with manicured flower-beds, elegant benches, neat, symmetrically patterned paths. Others, the larger ones in particular, are often close to nature, with winding paths, outcropping boulders, big, beautiful trees. City parks bear traces of modern life: ice-cream and hot-dog stands, balloon vendors, trash containers. A city skyline, with tall buildings and church spires, may be visible above the trees at the edge of the park. These elements should be carefully observed, and included in your park sketches for diversity and interest. Amusement parks are even richer in variety; it is up to you to decide what is more interesting—the people or the surroundings, the background or the foreground. Pick out a few items as the center of attention and focus your eyes on them. Draw and paint these features with somewhat more detail than the rest of the setting, but make the final result a cohesive picture.

Sketch anything and everything—figures, objects, groups, individuals, children, adults, birds, animals, trees, mountains, rivers, rocks, buildings, bridges. Sketch objects in your home—a corner of a room, furniture, pots and pans, fruits and vegetables. No subject is too big or too small, too simple or too complicated for sketching.

Look at your sketches weeks, months, years later, again and again. Not only will they evoke memories, but they will teach you, eventually, how to evaluate your own work. Your skill is bound to grow with every sketch, and so will your enjoyment in achieving mastery of the pastel medium. The faster and better you can sketch, the more time you will have for truly creative painting.

S. Carter 1951
N.A.

S. Lorka 1958.
N.A.

S. Croker N.A.
1958

S. Croke
1957